Patri

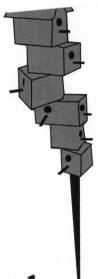

Crooked Little
Birdhouse

Random Thoughts on Being Human

For Karen, Chloe and Emily,
my not-so-small wonders

Contents

Crooked Little Birdhouse

No pessimist ever discovered the secret of the stars, or sailed to an uncharted land, or opened a new doorway for the human spirit.

~ *Helen Keller*

Before

THERE is a tree in my backyard. It's the perfect shade tree, broad and leafy; a thick canopy that protects the house from the setting sun's piercing rays.

It is the ideal place for a hammock; right under the kitchen window so you can chat with someone as they do dishes or make dinner, free of direct sunlight all day. It doesn't obstruct the yard so the children can play freely. But, should they see me in that hammock, it will no longer be mine alone. Anything a parent tries to keep for themselves becomes that which a child wants most.

Though I could surely trace it back further in my life, for simplicity's sake, it was in this hammock that I became a writer.

"What would you really want to be if you could be anything?" It's a question people ask each other when weather, sports, politics and personal hygiene have been exhausted, and they strive for a deeper topic. It refers to the perfect job in your opinion, not to your choice of superhero, wild animal or historical figure. Oftentimes the person is asking this only so they can tell you that they have the perfect job, that they are in the envious state of symbiotic peace in their lives and they want to make sure you know that they are ahead of you in the human race. These are the people you "ignore" friend requests from on Facebook.

When we get asked this question we slip into a fantasy world and try on different uniforms to see what fits. We search to find the illusion we feel would be the most blissful, contented and rewarding life. When friends would ask me this question throughout my life, I would always tell them I wanted to be a writer. Except during my first year of community college; in my first semester I wanted to be a marine biologist. In my second semester, a philosopher. And both still sound pretty awesome to me.

The odd thing about my desire to be a writer was this: I had done virtually nothing to make that dream a reality. Sure I'd occasionally make a note to myself about something I thought would be a good idea for a book; I'd keep journals of my rambling thoughts while travelling. At one point in my early twenties I even carried a personal tape recorder in my truck so I could capture every amazing, life-affirming and humanity-lifting thought I had no matter where I was, for use in a brilliant tome at a later date. But that later date got later and later.

While this may seem like I was making an effort to become a writer, I really wasn't. I did all that, but I did not actually write; never really sat down and put pen to paper or fingers to keyboard to expel the thoughts in my mind in a coherent manner. Notes and quips and thoughts and ruminations, sure. But I never wrote.

So when friends heard me say I wanted to be a writer, they would nod approvingly, and knowingly say things like, "Yeah, I could see you doing that." Then they'd deal another hand of Texas Hold 'Em or go to the fridge for another beer.

I was the only one of my mother's children to graduate college. It took seven years, but I have the degree from California State University, Northridge film school to prove it. This qualified me to be unemployed for six months until I was offered a job as the assistant to a movie producer who manufactured more bills at swanky Beverly Hills shops than actual movies. But I was grateful to be working in the field of my education. All those years of studying Griffiths and Wells, Truffaut and Fellini, and now I could put my talents to use answering the phone and telling the salesmen from Neiman Marcus that Suzette was unavailable right now even though she was sitting at her desk filing her nails, deeply engrossed in Vogue magazine. But the real use of my artistic skills came when I was sent to the pharmacist to pick up her prescriptions, or when getting her vintage corvette filled with gas.

Yes, I was living the dream.

But, as things in life always do, this one job led to another, and another, and after some years I evolved into a respected working professional in the post-production field, a technical area of film-making devoted to fixing everything that went wrong while film-makers were actually shooting their masterpieces.

I was content. I travelled occasionally, made decent money and a lot of very good friends. But I was never fulfilled, never felt like I was contributing something to mankind, my legacy or even the local economy. I was moving through this work and life in a state of "okay-ness." Not living to what I thought was my potential, but also not living beneath it. And this is going to sound like some fortune cookie or bubble gum wrapper wisdom. But I knew there was something more for me to do in this world. Or at least that was a gnawing feeling in my gut during my rare moments of self-awareness. It's not an uncommon feeling; I think most everyone suffers from it hypochondriacally. But, it is a hackneyed, overused human emotion that most people roll their eyes over; something we subscribe to in order to give our lives a little more meaning. It's the carrot we dangle before ourselves or target we aim at even if we never take the shot.

But there it is.

Back to the hammock.

One day almost 20 years into my career, and finally starting to enjoy some of the fruits of such longevity, I decided to take the day off for no other reason than to write something. A "creative health" day, if you will. The wife was out of the house, the kids in school. It was a lovely Southern California fall morning. Which is to say, achingly pleasant with not much variation from any other day in any other season.

I wasn't going to unearth my travel journals or tape-recorded burps of wisdom and finally get that great American novel out of my head in one day. No, I decided I was going to write about the municipal bike path. I hear Hemingway started the same way.

I've never been able to figure out whether Burbank, California, is a small city or a large town. Home to some of the largest film and television studios in the world, it has been my home since 2005. What you hear most about Burbank is this: good schools, good place to raise a family. And that's all we needed to hear. Cradled between the San Gabriel and San Fernando valleys of suburban Los Angeles, Burbank, like few other large towns or small cities, is stuck in its own time warp. Certainly it's been touched by drugs, gangs and crime like any other metropolis. But there is an overriding sentiment towards good old-fashioned family values that permeates life here.

3

We shop at the major retail chains that fill our malls, but favor the "mom and pop" shops that have eked out a living for decades. We take great pride in our family owned and operated coffee shops where everyone is a regular and the same waitress has served generations of families. The lifelong citizens are as ravenously defensive of their hometown as they are critical of it when the winds of change blow through -- like when a bike route cuts through the heart of their city.

There's the hills and the flats. Money buys you a house in the hills. Anything else lands you in the flats. But they are both bucolic and lovely places to live. Great care is taken by the city to maintain a lush, green umbrella of trees on all our city streets.

Minutes away from the beach, downtown L.A. and the mountains, Burbank is humble, and proudly so. Blue collar, unglamorous, striving for simplicity and comfort from one day to the next. Happiest when the world moves on around her. A supremely average American town.

I'd been reading in the local newspaper that there was some controversy about the newly installed bike path bisecting the town on a stretch of retired railroad tracks. The city received funds to beautify the unused railway and create a thoroughfare for bikers and walkers. A benevolent and worthy civic venture, if you ask most people.

Alas, there were those who found the spindly roots of discontent in even this. People wrote in to the newspaper complaining about walkers taking up space in the bike lanes; bikers dangerously veering into the walking lane. More volleys came from those who were shocked at the speed of said bikers even within the biking lane. Speed limits were demanded, police should be taken off vice and criminal duties in order to supervise the two-wheeled terrorists and walking wicked. There were angry calls to repave and repaint it to make it safer for all. There were reports of accidents and near accidents between those on bikes, scooters and foot. Indeed, one would get the impression this pleasant little bike path was the strip of embattled concrete separating North from South Korea.

So it was on this heated subject that I chose to write on my creative health day. It was a simple essay I can summarize thusly: "Seriously, folks?"

It felt good to sit and write, to say to myself and the world, "this is my writing time." It was cathartic to have the desire, the idea and eventually the completed work. But, while writing for oneself is a wonderful release and a creative endeavor worthy of its own rewards, to write begs being read. Ultimately, that is the purpose of communicating through the written word: to offer one's feelings with the rest of the world and embrace others in our shared human condition. The written word should provoke and appease; give voice so others may find commonness of thought and spirit and feel uplifted or justified.

So I emailed my little diatribe to the editor of the newspaper, not really thinking they would publish it. It wasn't a salacious rant, wasn't a true letter to the editor. It was too philosophical and not newsworthy. Just one man's rhapsodizing.

But, they called me a couple days later and told me they would publish it the next day.

And I won't lie. It was a huge thrill and ego boost to see my name and words in print, knowing they had been dropped on the driveways of thousands of people for use as a birdcage liner.

But I was hooked.

Two days later I received a surprising call from one of the editors. Did I happen to have another short essay lying around I could give to him right now? He was up against a deadline and some other contributor's letter didn't pan out.

I raced home from work and unearthed an essay I'd scribbled about the movie business for a company newsletter. I dusted it off, cut it down and sent it in. It ran the next day.

Published twice in one week! I was on a roll.

With this wind beneath my wings I sat down one evening and wrote a third piece, again not inflammatory, newsworthy or even informative for that matter. And I sent it in.

A week went by and I heard nothing. So I thought my run was over. My 15 minutes of fame expired in 500 words or less on the community forum page of my local newspaper. I was a little sad, but glad I had this opportunity. Sure, I might write some things down in the future and send them in, but it was time to get back to my real work and put this brief episode behind me.

But, a week later I received a voicemail saying this:

"Hi, Patrick, this is the editor from the newspaper. Hey listen, the other editors and I have really enjoyed the three pieces you've sent in recently. We were wondering if you'd like to have your own weekly column."

And this, ladies and gentlemen, is how a newspaper columnist is created. No diploma needed, no formal training in journalism. No certification, application, background check or blood test.

While it more accurately speaks to the murky talent pool available to local newspapers and the highly suspect taste of their editors, I like to think of this as divine intervention. My own Schwab's Drug Store moment; plucked from obscurity, the hand of fate and destiny descending from heaven, pointing its imposing finger at me and announcing to the world, "this lowly, unknown creature I have bestowed with an envious gift!"

Finally, a public forum for my delusions of grandeur.

When I met with the editor the following week, I did everything I could to dissuade her, to make her understand that I was not a writer, reporter or valid public voice worthy of a section in the newspaper once each week.

She brushed me off while simultaneously watching CNN on the television above her desk and listening to the police radio scanner behind her. She was undaunted.

"Just do what you've done with the last three pieces you sent us and you'll be fine."

"But one each week sounds like a lot," I pleaded. "Could we maybe do it once or twice a month?"

"No."

Newspaper folks don't waste a lot of time, I would come to find.

With that, she sent me down the hall to have my picture taken for the headshot that readers would come to visually associate with the opinions below it. Great. I wouldn't even be able to remain anonymous from the disgruntled readers I'd run into at the super-market. Luckily the headshot bears little resemblance to me. Or so I'm told.

One month later my first column ran, and I was obligated to deliver one each week until the editors and readers discovered I really didn't know what I was doing.

And I am still waiting.

I could write now. Not only did I have permission to write, but an obligation to. It was no longer just a wish or something to dream about when we have a bad day at the office. I now had the professional opinion of these editors that I could actually string words and sentences together in a coherent and intriguing manner fit for public consumption. It felt good to have strangers tell you that you can do this, even if you never believed it yourself. And still don't.

The fact that other people had more faith in me than I had in myself speaks of a common character flaw I share with, I believe, just about every sane, right-thinking human being. If you don't believe you have this personal quirk, you probably have it worse than the rest of us.

For the first few months I tried out various voices as I struggled to find my own as a writer and columnist. Funny, poignant, sad, angry, philosophical. I didn't like following local politics, city hall or many other community affairs, so I had little to say on these subjects. I was sure each week I'd open the paper to see my space filled by someone else. Or just a big blank area with an editor's note stating, "We're sorry. Patrick Caneday was a fraud unfit to print, even in this newspaper. We feel empty newsprint is more interesting than whatever he had to say this week."

But I eventually found that what people really wanted to read about, or at least what their feedback implied, were people. It didn't matter what I wrote about, so long as the readers could see it through the prism of a person: a homeless stranger, my favorite grocery store clerk, my kids, my family or even public figures. Give the reader a human being to tell a story through, and it didn't matter what the story was. When I had no one else to write about, I started exposing my own feelings, what I was thinking, enjoying or suffering through at any given time. I could be sad, angry, joyous or melancholy; I could vent deeply, deeply painful human emotions and struggles. And somehow this let people know they were not alone. They wanted to see themselves in someone else's story and be affirmed by that.

All the while, I was still working full time. I'd stay up late at night or get up early in the morning in order to get my weekly column in. And the newspaper kept taking it, much to my surprise.

After about nine months, the editors decided to run my column in another nearby local newspaper. Bordering Burbank to the east is Glendale, the city I was born and raised in.

If I can't tell whether Burbank is a small city or a big town, I can say with certainty that Glendale is a city. Not as large as Los Angeles, whose envious skyscrapers are visible from just about everywhere in Glendale to the north, but a city nonetheless; its own metropolis in the shadow of the City of Angels. A confused city struggling to maintain its own charm and individuality, yet so enamored by L.A.'s stature. And like it's older sibling, Glendale has become a melting pot for the Diaspora of world cultures: Armenian, Mexican, Korean, Greek, Vietnamese and more. Cuddled into the foothills of the San Gabriel Mountains, Glendale is a resting spot for so many vibrant nationalities. But, as happens when so many disparate groups gather in one place, they begin to isolate themselves. Sectarianism is one of Glendale's great tragedies; differing peoples growing farther away from each other rather than toward each other. I guess in that respect it's a lot like the rest of the world.

Though she suffers from this malady, Glendale does benefit from the colors of so many cultures. When a city works right, its people come to know the best of each other and the history they bring with them. As a child playing on her streets and in her hills, I grew close to people from all walks of life, and I think I'm better for it. Or at least I hope I am.

Glendale has its home-grown shops and cherished traditions, yet mourns them less when they disappear. She favors growth and status with her famous and infamous shopping malls, her coveted hillsides being stripped to make way for mini mansions. She wants the best of both worlds, the quaint and the extravagant. But she's yet to realize she's already lost the former. The Glendale of my mind is the one I've seen in faded, sepia tone pictures; cable cars and men wearing dashing hats helping ladies in billowy dresses to board them. A town that relished being a respite for those wanting to get away from the bright lights of the big city to her south. Glendale has a heart, but it's not on a map or even in words. Somewhere deep within her is that pulse for something lost, something simpler. It still exists, I believe. You just have to look a little harder to find it.

So, now writing for my hometown and my adopted hometown, I started to feel like I had a handle on this. I was getting comfortable as a writer.

And then I got fired.

Not from the newspaper, but from my regular, full time job. Laid off, more accurately, along with a few dozen other people at a company knocking on bankruptcy's door. It should have been a great shock, a devastating blow to someone who was used to being the breadwinner of the family. And it was a terrible crisis to so many of the good people I worked with. But, if truth be told, something deep within me wanted this; wanted it because it forced upon me something I don't think I could have ever done if left to my own feeble will power.

Write.

Write more.

With my newfound time, and the blessings of a generous, supportive, working wife, I decided to pour my energy into my creative efforts; to see if I could make something of it, earn something more than the price of two movie tickets each week -- which was roughly what I got paid for the column. Matinee tickets at that. This was the beginning of what I call my sabbatical year. A 12-month period in which I would devote myself to being a writer, even going so far as to call myself a writer when asked my profession, rather than an unemployed post-production executive.

This meant more time at home, more time with the family and more time with myself.

In fact, it meant a lot more than I ever could have possibly imagined.

Ever.

While sitting at my favorite coffee house one day early in my sabbatical, I ran into a friend. We talked about his work -- he's a graphic designer -- and mine; two people trying to make a living at independent, creative vocations. Business was steady for him, which meant a steady income and the contentment that comes with doing your job well and providing for your family. My work was steady as well, but only in the fact that the column was still running in the newspapers with positive feedback and appreciation from readers and editors alike.

My friend went his way, and I went back to my writing. He emailed me later that day and said something about appreciating people who try to reinvent themselves half way through their lives; people who leave one profession to pursue a more fulfilling one in hopes their leap of faith into something different, scary and perhaps irresponsible, would pay off.

"It seems like you're in the same boat as Gauguin and other late-blooming artists," he told me.

I took this as an unworthy compliment, but one that touched me deeply nonetheless.

I went back to work and then remembered something. Didn't Gauguin abandon his family and die of syphilis, penniless on a tropical island, blind and unable to see the beautiful scenery around him or even what he was painting?

This is where the adage "Be careful what you wish for. You just may get it," comes in.

When I said I wanted to be a writer, I had no idea what that truly meant. I wish now I'd been a little more specific.

As I said, I am not a journalist. Though I write for a newspaper, I never set out to be a reporter. The more I write, the less I even feel like a columnist. I consider myself an essayist, a chronicler of what it's like to be human as seen through (mostly) my own view of the world; someone who has random thoughts about life and puts them down for others to read and contemplate in short bursts. What follows in this book are many of the newspaper columns I've written over the last two years, reader favorites and my own favorites. There are also longer bursts, introductory essays to each chapter that allow me to explore the underlying theme of each chapter: Wonders is about the little things in life we may take for granted; Spirit explores faith and spirituality; Rivers ponders moments when there is an undeniable shift in life's course. Read it as a collection of essays if you want. Or see it as one human being struggling with being human. Either way, I hope you see something of yourself in these pages. And I hope you find that worthwhile. Because we all have a story to tell.

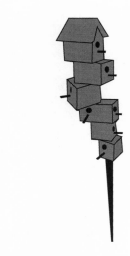

Wonders

Life is what happens to you
while you're busy making other plans.

~ *John Lennon*

That's better than a poke in the eye
with a sharp stick.

~ *My Mother*

Perfection

THERE is a concrete slab on a hill above Glendale, California, the city I was born and raised in. It rests among the scrub brush about 100 feet down a dirt trail, off a winding stretch of empty road between two hillside housing developments; the kinds of homes that have three floor plans to choose from times 400 houses and two feet between each of them. They are perfectly lovely, hermetically designed homes, if you like that sort of thing.

I discovered this slab accidentally on purpose. It was during that youthful, post-college-pre-family time of life when I thought I'd figured out the key to contentment. Indeed I thought I had the answers to life's most eternal questions. And the answer to everything was this: chasing sunsets.

It had just rained and the late day skies were clearing, yet wispy clouds remained, smeared in broad, uneven strokes overhead. Optimal conditions for a truly amazing sunset. The rains wash away the day's pollution, allowing the truest crystalline blue dome to reappear briefly over Los Angeles. But it's the clouds that make a sunset come to life; not the sky or the sun itself. As the sun inches below them on its way to the horizon, clouds become like mirrors reflecting every fraction of light the sun can give. It's said no human can look into the face of God. Indeed, even Moses had to look away in his presence, only to have God pass by him like a shadow. And that's what a good sunset is like. You don't actually see it by looking directly at the sun; you see how magnificent it is by the colors playing on the canvas of clouds. Colors no palette, camera, or words can properly capture.

These were the conditions shaping up on this particular day. So I grabbed a cheap bottle of red wine, some cheese and a dry salami from Trader Joes, and hit the road. I knew I had to get to an elevation high enough to see beyond the Verdugo Hills and the Santa Monica Mountains beyond them to the west. And I knew I didn't have much time if I wanted to see the whole show.

I don't know how many other places I drove by before finding the right one. On camping trips, I've been known to pass up six or eight perfectly good campgrounds before finally coming to rest in the one that "felt" just right. It's important to be really sure your location is right when the perfect storm of sunset conditions is converging. You want as wide a view as possible. It should be a quiet place, free of traffic, businesses and homes; a place where you can feel the stillness; where passersby are infrequent, but respectful when they do happen by. The kind of people who shoot you a knowing glance when they see you sitting there, staring into space, waiting and watching. These are rare places in the city, to be sure. But they are out there. And on this day I found one.

Up the hill, past the sprawling housing complexes with names like Via Vista, Via Verde and Via Bonita, and continue until you can look west unobstructed. There were no other cars parked nearby. A good sign. No fences or gates or warning signs -- just a hillside with an as-yet undeveloped view of the horizon. A fire road cut into the landscape providing a hiking trail for those who chose to find it. I walked down the trail a short way before coming upon the concrete slab -- a circle about ten feet in diameter and raised some 18 inches off the ground. Too small to be an emergency helicopter landing pad, too big to be a manhole cover. In fact, I've never been able to figure out what its purpose is. And I don't really care to know.

But there it sat seemingly out of place on this otherwise uns-carred hillside, a view south into downtown Los Angeles with its glass monoliths scratching the sky; north into the Angeles Crest Forest foothills with Montrose, La Cañada and La Crescenta, tucked into the trees and long sloping apron of land streaming down from the mountains; west into Burbank and the San Fernando Valley beyond.

I unfolded my chair, poured myself some wine, and waited for the show to begin.

And needless to say, I was not disappointed.

To call the colors pink, golden and orange doesn't do them justice. Salmon, amber and honey get closer, but still fall short and require adjectives I haven't learned yet. The world is bathed in such richness of light you can feel it satisfying you deep inside.

The way ice cold chocolate milk hits you deep in your maw and makes everything better. You see it on the clouds; you feel it on your face. You don't want to blink for fear of missing any of this slowly unfolding.

But one of the most important things to remember about sunsets is that you should occasionally look away. Avert your gaze briefly to the buildings, the hills, from time to time and see how they look in this glow. Then look back to the sky and clouds. Two, maybe three seconds is all that's needed. And you see just how greatly, and how subtly, the colors have changed in just those few seconds. Like a miracle unfolding before your eyes that you can't see until you're distracted.

You watch until the sun creeps below the land and sea a million miles away; then just a few minutes more, until grey consumes the world once again.

On that day and many more thereafter, I sat on that small slab of level concrete, my perch, watching the sunset, feeling like the axis on which the world turned. The center, the stillness in the tumult.

This was one of the ways I thought I could capture Perfection; harness what poets, musicians, philosophers and seekers have been trying to capture for millennia, and live every moment of every day in Zen-like unity with it.

And I was right.

And I was wrong.

It was a naïve pursuit, chasing sunsets. But it was something that gave me piece and fulfillment like nothing else during this time while I was waiting for other, unknown things to fill the void. Those moments of being so close to the light would be washed away as soon as I left the hill, got on the freeway and went home; when I woke up the next day to go to a job I didn't really care about, doing things I didn't really want to do. I'd try to recapture this feeling by sitting in the bed of my truck and eating lunch in a parking lot with a view of a smoggy and congested Hollywood, reading a book, listening to Bach. I'd try to force myself out of my physical surroundings and into bliss. For just a few minutes. Sometimes it worked. But usually it didn't.

I call it naïve not because those moments weren't real, not because I don't believe now that I was tapping into something meaningful and perhaps getting under the surface of a confused and short-sighted world. No. It was naïve because something in me thought it might be possible to live every moment in the light, to orchestrate a life lived in that Perfection in every way.

I don't know where this desire and impulse came from, nature or nurture. I didn't subscribe to any guru, yogi, healer or medicine man. Sure, I'd always been a dreamer. As a child I'd build elaborate make-believe worlds around me, but no more than anyone else. I remember lying awake at night fantasizing how cool it would be to have a light saber and Indy's bullwhip, and rescue that cute girl in 8th grade algebra from hooligans in the alley behind the gym during the school dance with the entire student body watching.

Didn't everyone?

I was never a good reader in school. Not even through college. I never buried myself in my room and visited the far off places of imagination crafted by Barrie or Tolkien. I got Boy's Life but only looked at the pictures. I lied to my 6th grade teacher about how many books I read in the class reading contest – a sin I would later admit to her in public. I read only what I absolutely had to, and even then I'd do whatever I could not to. Even Cliff Notes were a daunting task.

But somewhere in my early twenties that all changed, and I became a voracious reader. And the epiphany that inspired this change is something I am almost embarrassed to admit.

During the period after college graduation and before getting a job, the time when all of those people who swore they'd get you a job suddenly stop answering your calls, I was living at home, aimless and depressed. After scanning the newspaper every day for job openings and sending off desperate, incoherent letters to anyone and everyone in Hollywood asking for work, my day was filled with nothing.

There was a bookcase in my parents' house at the top of the stairs. And on its shelves were many books I'd never even bothered to look at. So one day, unable to muster the energy to go for a jog or find three dollars between the cushions of the sofa for a six-pack of plain wrap beer, I decided to look through the books, perhaps even read one. That's what I'd always been told books were meant for, so why not give it a try. At least it would fill the yawning, bleak time between waking and sleeping.

There were fat tomes by a guy named L'Amour, whimsical editions by some lady named Bombeck and rows of the collected comics of Calvin & Hobbes and the Wizard of Id. There were dog-eared bestsellers in paperback with cracked spines and even a handful of noble looking hardbacks some folks call "the classics." None of which seemed like what I needed right now.

Then I saw a slim little volume stuck between "The Autobiography of Malcolm X" and a bunch of half-completed "Mad Libs." Its undaunting size was immediately appealing. Dark blue, it was hardback and bore a title that sounded familiar, but I knew not why: "Jonathan Livingston Seagull."

I pulled it off the shelf and looked inside. The print was nice and large, not too many words on each page. It seemed wordy enough to make me feel like I was actually reading something of substance, but uncomplicated. I took it outside, sat in the sun and began to read.

Two hours later, I read it again.

Then once more before going to bed.

I think I may have read it the next day too, but I know I've read it a dozen times in the years since.

Sure, it was a slice of 1970's feel-good, pop philosophy. A fad, like tie-dye, pet rocks and the Scarsdale Diet. But this simple tale about a seagull that doesn't fit in resonated with me. I couldn't relate to this bird's drive, nor his aggressive seeking of some higher states of consciousness. I've never been hardwired with that kind of self-actualization. But I knew what he was looking for. Or at least had some vague notion. I knew there was something beyond the surface of things, a greater purpose if only we could get the chance to seek it out. I don't know how or why I felt this; can't explain it to this day. I'll save that for my therapist to figure out. But, I felt empowered and uplifted by this silly little book if for no other reason than it got me reading, opened a door for me that I'd never opened before.

And since that day, I've never gone a day without having at least one book I'm in the midst of. That book showed me there is a world in books I'd never even tried to tap into. And now that I was out of college, my reading list was my choice. I got to make my own syllabus. And ever since, I've been trying to tap into that feeling I got when I read about that wistful little seagull. I've found it on occasion over the years, but not every time, not every book.

Why just books, though? If I could get that feeling while reading, why not while watching a sunset, or driving up the coast with Peter Gabriel screaming on the tape deck? Or at home while making dinner? Or sitting at a bar, a baseball game, or alone at night with pen and paper?

My philosophy about life became this: there are three miracles in every day, the sunrise, the sunset and the third is there for you to find. Or create.

Finding people to share these emotions with was difficult. Like Jonathan, I felt misunderstood and out of place. When I talked about sitting on a hill and watching the sunset, or sitting in my truck bed at lunch time, I'd often get that crinkled-forehead, strained, curious look back from people. And still others seemed like they already knew what I was talking about and were bored with me; like I'd joined them at the game in the 5th inning and was trying to tell them what they'd already seen in the four innings before I arrived.

One day I got a voicemail from a co-worker and friend. She lived at the beach and was an avid runner. Her voicemail said this: "Hey, it's me. Just got back from a run on the beach. The sun was setting and it was awesome. It made me think of you. Just wanted to let you know that. See you later."

People still talk about how amazing our wedding was.

During the reception, a family friend asked me to step outside to talk to him. He was a man I only knew casually, but liked very much. He knew me only casually as well. We stepped out of the boisterous dining hall and into a perfect springtime evening tucked in the hills over Malibu.

And he said this to me: "There is a childishness to you, something innocent that doesn't really fit."

I was a little offended. I didn't really know what he was talking about. I was in my thirties by now. I was finally getting somewhere with my career. I had just gotten married, which seemed a pretty mature thing to do. We were serving brie en croûte, for crying out loud!

Then he said, "Don't ever lose that."

I knew he'd just complimented me, but I didn't know how.

This is just one example of what seems to be a universal issue in life. Namely, that we have opinions and images of ourselves that differ greatly from those others have of us. We don't have a clue what others see when they look at us, and it's impossible for us to see through their eyes. We can get a glimpse briefly, and when we do the experience can be enriching, debilitating or both; it can cause us to rise to some challenge with new self confidence or curl up in a ball on the futon gulping Two-Buck Chuck straight from the bottle.

And against my better judgment, against my own desires and efforts to the contrary, I've heeded his words. I've been unable to change that part of me. I'm still naïve, still think there are perfect answers to everything; still try to find those magical moments in life when the scales fall from our eyes and we're allowed to see things as they were truly meant to be. It is both fortunate and unfortunate, as I see it.

Back then I called it Perfection. I thought there was a formula for getting through each day as successfully as possible, seizing the carpe and diem and wringing it for everything it had; avoiding the pitfalls, the pain and the darkness that trapped so many others. I thought life was a recipe, and if you mixed the ingredients just right, kneaded it just so, let it rest, let it rise, you got the perfect loaf of crusty bread. And I wanted to share it with the world and say, "See! Perfection is possible in every moment, in every day!"

But that is simply not true. That's not the way life is supposed to be.

Perfection implied some state of being where everything is peaceful and harmonious in this blissed out, head-in-the-clouds way. Working, maintaining friendships, getting married, having children, surviving day-to-day, seeing loved ones suffer and die;

these were all parts of the journey, all things that bring both good and bad, suffering and joy. But I hadn't seen most of that yet. To think that life can be lived in perfect harmony is to miss out on what life is truly about. You can't have the resurrection without the crucifixion.

We need to not know what is going to happen in three days even if it scares the hell out of us. We need to get nicked and scraped and kicked in order to rise up again. It's scary but needed. Sometimes we have to accept that things don't have a perfect equation to provide the ultimate desired outcome. I don't like the nicks and scrapes, but I wouldn't know up if I weren't down.

It's the bruises and flaws in ourselves, our friends and lovers, in our society and world, that add the uniqueness to them. A little imperfection gives character to something that is already beautiful, intriguing or captivating. It's the hideous green carpet in your otherwise cute rental house that you eventually tear up and find a pristine hardwood floor underneath.

Certainly there are moments when everything falls into place; when the sun and the wind and the rain and the wine meet and intertwine to elevate an experience to new levels of visceral, cerebral and spiritual understanding. Times when you're holding her in your arms and slowly moving on the dance floor forgetting there are others nearby, and the only music is in your hearts. But I was wrong in thinking they could be captured and bottled. They can't. They can most certainly be relished though, in the moment we are in them, knowing more will come for those who are faithful.

Perfection was no longer adequate. I needed a new name for what I couldn't help but try to discover.

When I started writing a weekly newspaper column, I was challenged to "find my voice" as they say in writing circles. Some columnists write about politics or consumer advocacy or sports or the struggles of menopause. I wasn't qualified for any of that. I was told to go write five or six pieces in advance and we'd get started. I really had only one place to turn for material at the time.

"Daddy, today I am going to try buttons," my older daughter announced one day. She was six years old at the time and proceeded to take the rest of the day to do just that, soon discovering she could indeed button her own pants, shirts and sweaters all by herself.

Having children is both the greatest gift and punishment we can receive in life. It's the greatest gift because of all the discoveries we make by and about our children and ourselves. Sadly, it is the greatest punishment for the very same reason.

The rewards of parenthood come in those all-too-brief moments between the chaos and disasters when we do ourselves the favor of seeing life through their eyes. And when we do this, over time we see that their worlds expand outward concentrically as they grow. Life to the child is a never-ending discovery. Life to the adult is the discovery of the never-ending.

A newborn's world is but six inches in front of its face and no more. They grasp at strange sounds and blurry objects for the sole purpose of putting things in their mouths — Cheerios, pacifiers, beetles and breasts. A crawler's world extends out a few feet from the place he or she has been positioned; anything within this radius is fair play for slobber, destruction or joy. Walkers explore the room and the world more extensively, but only as far as the invisible apron strings from mommy and daddy allow.

When my daughters were little, the world they were allowed to discover extended south one house but no further than the invisible line drawn by the neighbor's hedge, and north three houses but not beyond "The Big Tree." That Big Tree was an ancient, gargantuan eucalyptus that would eventually be cut down by the city for safety reasons.

Seriously, this thing was enormous. I heard that The Big Tree once served as a landmark for pilots attempting to land at our local airfield. In the age of global positioning systems and Yahoo Maps, something about a physical marker seen from thousands of feet in the air makes me feel nostalgic, grounded and safe. I'll be honest, I'm a little lost without The Big Tree. I don't blame the city for cutting it down, though. In the last year, two branches, each alone bigger than the average oak tree, have come crashing down into the street. But I am sad to see The Big Tree gone. For my kids, the world now extends to The Big Hole and I hope not too far beyond that.

25

Curiosity is what drives us to push our boundaries out farther than we have before. An insatiable curiosity about what lies beyond our borders, both physical and metaphysical. And it doesn't hurt to have a dash of naiveté mixed in for those times when we're told we're searching in vain. Some pretty great discoveries have been made because someone didn't know any better.

I remember reading "Stuart Little" to my girls, one chapter each night when they were finally old enough to appreciate it. They sat quietly and listened as intently as their twitchy little bodies would allow. It was an experience I'd been waiting for since the day I found out I would become a father. As we read, their world expanded further into the limitlessness of their imaginations.

Stuart Little asked his young class, "How many of you know what's important?"

Up went all the hands.

"Henry Rackmeyer, you tell us what is important."

"A shaft of sunlight at the end of a dark afternoon, a note in music, and the way the back of a baby's neck smells if its mother keeps it tidy," answered Henry.

"Correct!" said Stuart. "Those are the important things. You forgot one thing though. Mary Bendix, what did Henry Rackmeyer forget?"

"He forgot ice cream with chocolate sauce!" said Mary.

"Exactly!" said Stuart

We are all very small mice on very big adventures. And life isn't about Perfection. It's about wonders. Small wonders. Each and every day.

As [Stuart] peered ahead into the great land that stretched before him, the way seemed long. But the sky was bright, and he somehow felt he was headed in the right direction.

Peter Pan and the Ice Cream Man

IT'S Sunday, we're home from church, and the neighbor kid my girls usually play with is out of town. The wife needs to study for the state nursing exams. The kids are so wound up their heads are about to pop off like those helicopter toys when you pull the cord. And I am stuck on 43 Across of the Sunday crossword puzzle.

It is the perfect storm of domestic disturbance calls.

Something had to be done. I thought long and hard about what was most important: a nursing license or my crossword puzzle. My marriage hung in the balance.

"Come on, kids," I proclaimed. "We're going to the library."

You would have thought I said, "Come on, kids. We're going to the proctologist." The reaction was about the same.

We had about 1,658 books to return. The library called asking whether we would like to return them or have people come to our house to check them out. I detected the kind of insane, sarcastic tone in the librarian's voice my mother used to get when she found out I had dropped out of yet another junior college class.

To my children, the two blocks from our house to the library is about as much fun to walk as the Green Mile. My punishment for making them take this trek of terror is this: They walk at half my pace and veer in front of me constantly, like bats with malfunctioning radar. Every three steps I trip over them, stop, let them get ahead, trip over them again and repeat. A walk like this takes 10 times longer than it should and usually ends in tears. First theirs, then mine.

Within sight of the library entrance, the unthinkable happened: ice cream truck music.

Before I knew it or had a chance to say no, we were standing in line behind another family as they placed their orders. There was a mother and father and several kids, the youngest wearing a Peter Pan costume. This seemed perfectly normal. His face beamed pixie-like when his father gave him his ice cream.

As my girls chose that, no that, no that, no that, I realized something that could possibly have affected my relationship with them for the rest of our lives. I had only $1 in my wallet.

Now when I was a kid, this would have bought me and three friends a Grab Bag, which would have made us happy for days. But today there is not much in the world that brings happiness for a buck despite what the fast food restaurants tell us.

When the family in front of us finished and moved on, I gathered my courage and humility and asked Mr. Ice Cream Man if he had anything for (gulp) $1 my daughters could share.

As Mr. Ice Cream Man gave us our choice between the thing he just scraped off the floor of his van or a couple spent Popsicle sticks from which they could suck any remaining juice, something completely unexpected and potentially even more humiliating happened.

Peter Pan's dad came back around the corner of the ice cream truck, wallet open, extending two dollars to me. My life literally flashed before my eyes.

This is not supposed to happen to me. I have a good job. I pay my bills. I am, occasionally, the guy that hands other people a couple bucks. It is not supposed to go like this.

"Here take it," he said.

"No," I insisted, waving him off. "No, no, it's OK."

But what I really wanted to do was show him my bank statement. It's not flush, but it is not empty. "I have money," I'd say. "I don't need a handout. I just don't have cash on me. You've mistaken me for someone less fortunate."

"Take it," he insisted back. "I've been caught without a couple bucks in my pocket before. Really. Take it." His hand with the bills in it was practically in my chest.

At Glendale High School a million years ago I had a Spanish teacher, Mr. Gallagher. We learned more about life than we did about Spanish in Mr. Gallagher's class. And one thing he taught us that I have never forgotten is this: When someone offers you a gift, take it. You are giving a gift back to them by doing so.

With a deep sigh, humbled yet again, I took the money from Peter Pan's dad. I thanked him sincerely and off he went. Out of the corner of my eye, I'm sure I saw Pan fly off giggling.

Now, flush with three dollars, I asked the girls what they wanted. Both picked an ice cream costing $2. Never fails.

The kindness of strangers has become a hackneyed term. But that may be because I have always tried to see myself as the stranger. While there is reward in that, I found it heartwarming to be the recipient of that simple, unexpected and random act of kindness. I hope Pan's dad did as well.

It was $2. But to my girls, sitting on the grass this warm winter day, it was the best ice cream they had ever had. There is no price great enough nor humiliation low enough for that.

January 24, 2009

∾❦∾

A Man and His Barbecue

THERE are mysteries in life that I will never be able to explain. The imagination of a child. A man's fascination with baseball and grilling meat. And the fact that virtually every main street in Burbank is in a continual state of road repair.

It's Saturday morning, which at our house means food. And SpongeBob. And gym class. And tantrums. And doodling on my ridiculous mug shot in the paper. And food.

By 9 a.m., I'll be daydreaming about what choice cut of beef to purchase at the Handy Market today.

Last week, the wife asked me in exasperation, "So, when are you finally going to get your new barbecue?"

Bingo.

For more than a year I've cajoled, begged, nudged and subtly hinted about my deep need for a new barbecue. A need not unlike oxygen. When friends come over, friends who have nicer grills than mine, I make sure the wife is within earshot when they tell me how pathetic my grill is. I leave hardware store ads around the house conspicuously open to the barbecue page. On family trips to the hardware store, I ogle the Webers, Char-Broils, Nexgrills and Per-fect Flames, while the kids collect paint samples for every color in the Disney home decor line. I'll find them later playing poker with them in the garden section with other latchkey kids.

And finally, I have the green light. Better yet, she brought it up, so it sounds like it was her idea. She fell right into my trap.

I've done the research online, compared prices, features and brands. Shopped Lowe's, Home Depot, Do-It Center, OSH and Barbecues Galore. I've lifted more lids than a toupee salesman.

I settled on the Master Forge 4 Burner LP Gas Grill. Burger count capacity: 40. Square inches of primary cooking surface: 827. BTUs: 52,000. Hours of cooking pleasure: limitless. Rotisserie burner, side stove-top burner, side searing burner. This last acces-sory seemed like a gimmick. I've never seen it on another grill. I usually don't fall for these gimmicks, but it is so cool!

They offered free assembly, but that would take two days. They offered to let me take one of the previously assembled models that are chained together in front of the store collecting dust. A sucker's barbecue. No, this is a project a man needs to do for himself.

It was a beautiful spring day, the kind of day that reminds you summer is right around the corner. Sunny, but not hot. Breezy, but not cold. Radio on, the kids playing next door and thankfully unavailable to "help" me build the barbecue. The wife sat nearby, soaking up the sun, utterly relaxed.

I opened the box and spread the parts all over the yard to keep them organized. Carefully, I surveyed the task, then dove in swiftly, allowing the meditation of the build to possess me. Don't rush; take your time with each and every screw, washer and cotter pin. It was a timeless moment of sheer masculine contentment. Slowly, gently, my creation came to life.

When I finished, I pulled out my old, feeble grill and set it side by side with my new one. So embarrassing. I averted my eyes. It was a leper compared to the beauty that was my new barbecue.

When I suggested Porterhouse for dinner, the king of steaks, the wife told me to slow down. Don't be so aggressive. She's a new grill. Take your time, get your feel, find the hot spots. See where she flares up and where she goes cold. It takes two to grill right. You can't force her secrets out of her. You've got to finesse them out. Make her sing. If your barbecue is happy, you'll be happy.

Wise, wise wife.

We went with rib-eyes for the inaugural meal.

You have one shot to cook a steak to perfection lest that cow gave its life in vain. And I don't want that on my conscience. Men have a need to cook outdoors and provide meat for their families. Maybe it's just the ever-present potential for an explosion when dealing with contained gases and fire. But I think it's something more.

When the kids finally came running back into the yard, they gasped. I smiled proudly. My kids know quality grillware when they see it.

"Cool!" they cried. "Look at that huge box!"

And that huge box would soon become a car, a plane, a boat, a castle and a spaceship. Off they went to other worlds.

As I flipped the steaks, I let the soothing voice of Vin Scully take me into the night of my own dreams. Dreams of open roads, Porterhouse steaks and happy children.

April 18, 2009

❦

A Day in the Life of Dad

AFTER a couple of gut-wrenching rounds of rock-paper-scissors, it was decided that my wife would be the one staying home when we started having children. Each day as I left the house for work she would say to me, "There will be a time when I'm working and you will have to take care of the kids all day." As children wailed in the background, her desperate cling to sanity was lost on me.

Until now.

As she kissed me goodbye and skipped gleefully away from the house one recent Saturday morning, I thought, "How hard could it be?" Then, while my two daughters began their daily Sponge-Bob SquarePants marathon, the scope of the day's itinerary came over me like a dark cloud: breakfast, get dressed, gym class, change clothes; five year old's birthday party, lunch, home, change clothes; eight year old's birthday party, change clothes; market, dinner, change clothes; play, bathe, pass out. Change clothes.

While the kids readied themselves with a breakfast of champions -- milkless Frosted Flakes, a glass of strawberry milk and a turkey sandwich -- I mentally and physically prepared myself. Using Map-Quest I charted our course to find every coffee house, Jamba Juice, public restroom, police station and child protective services office on our route. I put on my favorite cargo pants; the extra storage would be needed to carry the toys, tissues, trash, half-eaten candy and any severed body parts the day would bring. I did a few sets of deep knee bends while holding a 50 pound sack of potatoes. Packed some snacks, water, extra underwear (mine and theirs) and we hit the road.

Gym class is a safe warm up to the day — calisthenics before the race ahead. I ask to join their class, but am denied by their spunky 16-year-old instructor. If I pull a hamstring today, I'll know who to blame.

Afterward we have 20 minutes to change clothes and get from Burbank to the Glendale Galleria. When it comes to life skills, teaching one's children to change clothes in the car cannot be undervalued. Right up there with dialing 911 when Daddy is about to use power tools.

We arrive at Build-A-Bear Workshop with just seconds to spare. Twenty gleeful and sugar-deprived five year olds are running in circles as the gate opens. Quickly the store employees wrangle the kids into breathless obedience. This being the first party of the day, the clerks are friendly and chipper, but I fear for them by mid-afternoon.

They begin leading the children through a series of steps to build their own teddy bear. If you've never been to Build-A-Bear, think Frankenstein and sausage casings. First, the kids are given a soulless, unstuffed shell of a bear. Next there is a somewhat disturbing séance in which small, dormant hearts are awakened prior to being placed inside the bear. The procedure culminates with the bear being injected with stuffing from a device that would make Willy Wonka blush.

As the kids are pampering their new babies, picking out names and designer clothes for them, I have a moment to wander off for a cup of coffee and a quick chat with other parents. These are the kinds of conversations that have no beginning and no end — too quickly we are called to address some new crisis.

"No, I don't think the Gucci handbag goes with that Vera Wang gown and Liz Klein shoes."

"Yes, I think your 17 other Build-A-Bears will get along quite nicely with Becky Bear even if she does look oddly like Dick Cheney."

When the festivities end, we march off to get pizza. I look over my shoulder as we leave the store and see the birthday girl's mother sobbing at the cash register, her trembling hand offering up several credit cards. I feel a twinge of guilt as I realize I don't even know what present we got for sweet little...um...

"Hey girls, whose party is this?"

We race home for the obligatory midday changing of clothes and then head off to our next party back in Burbank. As we pull up to party No. 2, my worst fears are realized. Outside on the lawn are six angelic little girls dressed in their Sunday's finest, sitting properly with bonnets atop their heads and pinkie fingers pointing skyward. That's right: tea party.

I offload the girls as I look for parking and toy with the idea of bolting. "I fell asleep in my car," I would say to excuse myself when I picked them up. But once you play the narcolepsy card, you have to stick with it for years to come.

The girls eat crumpets and play with costume jewelry; make butterfly crafts and decorate picture frames. I reach for a bottle of cheap tequila and am handed a raspberry infused organic green tea with mint sprig in a fine China cup and saucer. While I sip, I lapse into a state of transcendental meditation and I'm sitting in a dingy bar near Chávez Ravine, arguing about Manny Ramirez and picking a fight with a Hell's Angel.

At day's end my mind is mush. The only thought in my head is this: When the hell did "cha cha cha" become a part of the lyrics to "Happy Birthday to You?"

We get home just in time for the sugar tremors to set in. I muscle the girls into their straitjackets, shove wooden spoons in their mouths and turn on the TV.

"Who lives in a pineapple under the sea..."

Coffee: $4. Toys: $53. Bail: $900. A day spent with the kids learning what stay-at-home parents go through: $2,798.

Sorry. Priceless, that's what I meant. Priceless.

May 23, 2009

☙

On Shoes, Romance, Commencement and the Big Picture

I LOVE a good pair of boots.

About a month ago I went to the Red Wing Shoes in Magnolia Park and purchased a new pair to replace the beaten ones I've had for more than 10 years. This made me think about that dreamy, weepy book "The Bridges of Madison County," which made me think about the author, Robert James Waller. This made me think about romance and the fact that I was not asked to speak at any commencement ceremonies this graduation season.

Welcome to my brain.

Follow me.

I am not so proud as to hide the fact that when "The Bridges of Madison County" came out in the early '90s, I fell for it hook, line and sappy sinker. Didn't everyone? I let it carry me off to the idyllic backcountry of Iowa, and I wept when it became clear these lovers could never be together. If you are new to this column, exposing the most embarrassing moments of my life is what I do here.

In his book, Waller describes the rugged main character, Robert Kincaid, wearing well-worn Red Wing field boots. This stuck with me because there's always been something nostalgic and trusted about Red Wings for me; I picture the red-winged symbol in small towns all over America.

The shoes — like their wearers, I imagined — are strong, long-lasting and sturdy; comfortable and made with great care and attention to detail by people who appreciate good footwear. They aren't cheap, but they're worth it. If there is one thing in your wardrobe not to skimp on, it's your shoes. You will do much walking in your life, and it's crucial to be comfortable and confident where your feet hit the ground.

So taken was I with this book, I searched for anything else Waller had written and came across a speech he gave to a graduating college class. The speech was titled "Romance" and fairly well summed up a worldview I happen to agree with.

Waller talked about romance as something that can't be directly defined. But it's that which "makes all the living and doing you are so anxious to get on with worthwhile." It's not exactly the same thing as the sense of love between two people, but it's certainly present in that. Romance "fuels your life and propels your work with a sense of vision, hope and caring."

When I was in high school and there was nothing to do — which seemed like every moment of a teenager's life — my friends and I would drive up the winding foothill roads, find a spot to park and look out over the city. One of our favorite vista points gave us a panoramic view over Glendale to the east and Burbank to the west. The multicolored lights glistened from the heat of the valley floor, hypnotizing us. It was our first big-picture view, and romance was there.

It's that feeling you get when you come through the tunnel connecting the 10 Freeway and Pacific Coast Highway and you turn your car up the coast, born anew from city to ocean, with sea gulls urging you northward. Or when you cross the desert on an open road with the windows down and Peter Gabriel howling on the stereo. Romance is with you when you're mountain biking or exercising or playing basketball and feel like nothing can stop you. It's the sensation you get with your loved one, or on a first date, when a smile says more than a thousand words.

Romance hates crowds, and she doesn't like to be looked at directly. She's all around you, not out there somewhere else. She's dancing "just beyond the firelight, in the corner of your eye." And she can be chased away easily.

She abhors over-analysis, obsessive neatness or excessive focus on detail and procedure. She can't stand materialism or doing anything just for the money. Most top 40 music makes her hide, as do tabloid news and traffic. She has no tolerance for whining, complaining and self pity.

She's at the Tallyrand and Ben's Deli and the Handy Market, places that care more about people and doing simple things right than about profit margins and productivity reports. She's at the Starlight Bowl on a warm summer night with jazz in the air, floating on the sumac-scented breeze.

Romance is near when you're alone. I was in a small town on the Mediterranean coast of Italy once, standing atop a hill by myself overlooking the ocean. As darkness fell and the waves could no longer be seen, I found myself surrounded by thousands of fireflies.

Romance is there when you're with like-minded people. As we crested that last hill of the Inca Trail, we found ourselves staring down at the perfect postcard view of Machu Picchu. I don't think we breathed for half an hour as we took in the awesomeness of the ruins. Sometimes silence is the only suitable conversation, and not everyone understands that. My traveling partner that day would become my wife.

Surround yourself with people who have this passion. There will be enough unromantics in your life — miserly bosses, cranky co-workers and those people jockeying for free food at Costco. But if you have a good core group of Romantics to welcome you in from the rain, your soul will survive another day.

Romance was on that hill when I was 17. We may not have known it then, but she was there.

So, to those graduating from preschool to kindergarten, elementary to middle school and high school to college or the great beyond, I say this:

Live your life with passion and romance.

Stay grounded in who you are and what you believe.

Be humble, for you will make mistakes, and your opinions will not always be right.

Keep the big picture always in mind.

And if nothing else here speaks to you, at least trust me on the shoes.

June 6, 2009

❧

Stand in the Long Line

I FIND it interesting that in such a populous area we fight so hard to avoid one another. Or maybe it's just me, and you're all finding ways to get together without inviting me.

That's understandable.

But I have some advice for you. The next time you're feeling like an ogre, go shopping at the Pavilion's on Alameda Avenue in Burbank. Battle for a parking space. Go inside and find that you've forgotten your list, coupons and green bags. Crash carts with that lady who got the last L'Oréal Shimmering Color T53 hair treatment before you. Pick a dozen extra-large eggs that has only 11 good ones. Scream at your kids to get their hands out of the olive bar. Pick up some steaks and let the juice run down your arm and onto your pants. Smile through gritted teeth at the 23 clerks who will ask if you're finding everything all right today.

And once you've run that grocery store gauntlet, find the longest checkout line and stand in it. Chances are Barbara is the checker, and you'll never get into anyone else's line again.

I probably met Barbara a dozen times before I really met her. In a world where we interact with so many people on a daily basis yet know so few of them, she was just another checker at my local supermarket.

I was alone on this shopping trip. I don't remember what I bought and wasn't paying much attention to anyone around me. When it was my turn, the checker smiled broadly and acted as if we were long-lost friends.

"Hey! How are you? How are those two beautiful girls of yours?"

And I thought to myself, "Stalker?"

But no. This is Barbara. And she is about the friendliest person I've ever met. A warmth so sincere it's shocking; it jolts you from the walking coma you're in day by day. She's genuinely kind, effusive and warm, though she admits to being a little shy, which I don't believe.

Hers is not the corporate-mandated courtesy that clerks are forced to offer at supermarkets nowadays.

"No, I don't need help to my car today, thanks. It's just a pack of gum."

And it isn't just me. She's like this with everyone in her line and many who aren't. When it's your turn in Barbara's line, you just want to pull up a chair and stay for a while.

I sat with Barbara recently in the deli section of the store, selfishly taking up her time while she tried to eat a salad on her lunch break. The first question I asked her was, "What makes you so friendly?"

"I think it's just natural," she told me. "I think I get that from my parents. They were so nice and so good to us kids."

The only girl in a brood of five, Barbara had a great example set for her by her parents. Happily married for 53 years, her folks were active in the community and always available to their kids. Her father died six years ago, but her mom is still around to provide the kind of motherly love and no-nonsense support that kids of all ages need.

"And I'm a Christian," she added. "A lot of it is my faith. I think God watches over me and my son. I may not go to church every week, but I try to teach my son to treat people the way you'd like to be treated."

And it is for her 14-year-old son that she lives.

A really good day for Barbara is this: "Hanging out with my son, having a couple of his friends over and going to the park. I'll sit in the shade and watch them play baseball. Afterwards we'll order a pizza and I'm good to go. I don't need a lot of things. The best day is spending it with him."

And it's not just her own son who makes her happy. When I asked her what the best thing about her work is, she didn't hesitate.

"The kids," she said with peace and sureness in her voice.

She's so popular with them she gets invited to their birthday parties. "I see these kids grow up. That's the part I like. I get to know people."

She belongs at a local "mom and pop" market where she can say things like, "Do you want me to put that on your tab, Joe?" But I'm glad she's at my supermarket. She brings some humanity and personality to such a big, impersonal place.

From a management view, I'm sure long checkout lines are to be avoided. But to this regular shopper, that long line is the unequivocal sign of an incredibly valuable employee, a truly good person and the very reason I shop at this market.

A recent Harvard University study tells us that happiness is contagious. One's proximity to and frequent face-to-face interaction with happy people is fundamental to one's own happiness. That's something you can't get from texting, e-mailing or using the automated checkout.

Living simply, loving fully and giving the free gift of kindness to people. Money can't buy happiness, the cliché goes. But some clichés are true. Family, community, God, sunny days, kids playing ball, pizza and friends.

It's so simple. Which is probably why most of us don't believe it. Good thing we have someone like Barbara to remind us once in a while.

June 13, 2009

The Long View of Old Friendships

THERE are views that look out across great expanses of land. There are views that look out across vast stretches of time; past, present and future. And once every so often, if you're lucky, you find yourself in a place where you get both in the same moment.

I am so lucky.

Brit Trydal is a second mother to me. Not a stepmother or a mother in law, but a family friend known so long there isn't a place in my memory without her. She and my mother have been friends more than 40 years. In my lifetime our families have always lived across the street from each other.

On a recent balmy summer night with the heat of the day just vanishing over the San Gabriel Mountains, Brit's children threw a lavish tropical-themed party to celebrate their mother's 70th birthday. We were a block away when I heard ukuleles and the unmistakable cackling laugh of my mother, a sure sign the two ladies had found each other. It's the joyous laugh of old friends who've seen each other thousands of times, yet rejoice in it anew every time.

The backyard was converted into a lush island paradise; hand carved wooden idols, tiki torches and a bamboo bar serving Mai Tais whose recipe, I'm told, was smuggled from Damon's Steakhouse. The ladies in their prettiest dresses, the men in their tackiest Hawaiian shirts. The hilltop view spanning from the amber hills of La Crescenta down through the valley to the shimmering hills of the Los Angeles skyline.

Family and friends, young and old, gathered to celebrate a beautiful life. Little ones ran through the maze of adults, their goal to find the kind of adventure only found at grown up parties when parents are otherwise occupied. Parents sat back and relaxed, simply glad their children were also otherwise occupied. Once strong men in their winding down years were tended to by their loving wives, the truest testimony to love and the commitment of a lifetime. Later that night my wife would tell me that she would take care of me this way, when I am old and unable to recognize those I once knew well.

And through the night I heard that laugh over and over again. It's the laugh we heard from the kitchen when my mother and Brit shared their burdens with each other each evening. With dinner working on the stove, my mother would call Brit and ask, "Do you have time for a drink?" Her voice was half casual, half desperate. Within minutes the two ladies would be enjoying a "just a quick drink" while we children made mayhem around them.

Young children have a hard time seeing their parents at peace and happy. We demanded their attention in the same way my children now do when I sit to work at the computer or engage in an adult conversation or do anything but focus solely upon them. But these mothers were unflappable after years of rearing their young. "Go play," we were admonished with icy glares, while they took their well deserved respite.

It's during these daily briefings that lifelong friendships are solidified; friendships that don't judge or gossip; bonds that are strengthened by mere routine presence. There were tears and hard times. The trials of divorce, death and addiction among so many other struggles. The aching that parents feel so keenly when they see their children suffer, a pain worse than any inflicted upon oneself. Friendships like this are not about the moment, but the collection of moments. And they grow ever stronger as one puts more into that vessel of time.

They set an example for us, their children, for now there is no place in my life without Brit's daughters. And my children have never known a time without their children; generations of friendship gifted from parent to child to grandchild.

Boys and girls gathered close, as did a few men, to watch as hula dancers took the stage to become the wind, sea and sky in graceful motion. Children leaped at the chance to join in. Parents and grandparents beamed. The inevitable Conga line formed and I begrudgingly took part, cajoled by my wife. She just looked so pretty in that tropical dress. As I saw my mother approach the limbo bar, I grew fearful.

"Mom, you're going to break a hip!" I scolded her.

"Oh shut up," she retorted as she shimmied under.

And I was back in the kitchen of my youth.

41

From the youngest to the oldest, all were lives encapsulated in moments and memories. The troubles and pains of life had fallen off, as they will always do, and only the good remained.

Friendships are honed by the monotony of time, the repetitive grind of moving through days one at a time. And along the way, births and deaths, hurt and healing, coffee and booze, family vacations and fearful isolation. Cries of agony and cries of laughter.

When we are all blocks and miles and years away, remember the laughter. Always the laughter.

July 18, 2009

❧

Moments and Miracles

"You don't really understand human nature unless you know why a child on a merry-go-round will wave at his parents every time around — and why his parents will always wave back."
— Bill Tammeus

LET'S be honest. Parenting is hard. Most of the time you feel like you're just barely clinging to sanity, doing and saying things you never thought you would. Every rule and discipline you dole out is a roll of the dice. It's like investing in government bonds. You put your money in, but you can't see the benefit for 25 years until it matures.

But while we all wait for Morphine OTC to hit the market and give us some self-medicating relief, there are moments. Moments of pure, simple reward that give us just enough energy to keep going another day. If we still ourselves long enough to notice them, they will come.

Every parent is guilty of watching their child from outside the schoolyard fence. If not, you're cold and heartless, and need read no further. It's curiously dangerous and exciting to see them maneuver through the world unprompted; playing with others not knowing that Mommy or Daddy is nearby.

It was about 8 a.m. one recent morning, so the girls were on only their third wardrobe change of the day. A friend recently handed down a Dorothy dress from "The Wizard of Oz" to my five year old. It became the "daily dress," the one that gets worn every day, just not to school, church or the supermarket. She put it on and asked for pony tails to round out the look. Grabbing her mechanical walking dog, a scruffy cairn terrier, she set out to the front walk, her own Yellow Brick Road.

After a little while I got up to see what she was doing. The hazy morning light gave the whole scene a dreamlike tone. I saw her slowly walking her dog, its gears grinding and whirring, content and at peace until she saw a large earthworm in the middle of the path. She squatted down and inspected it with great interest. She turned the mechanical dog off and picked up a twig. Just as I thought she was going to impale the worm and smear it across the walk, she did quite the opposite. She gently poked it and prodded it, trying to get it off the concrete that would soon become a frying pan as evidenced by the multitude of dried worm carcasses nearby.

"Go," she whispered eagerly. "Hurry. Get into the grass. Go."

The earthworm fought her back, snapping and wriggling furiously. But she persisted in urging it into the safety of the lawn. Once it was safely burrowing into the cool ground, she stood, picked up Toto and gleefully skipped off down the sidewalk.

It was 6 a.m. on another morning, and I sat at my desk reading in the stillness of a home where not a creature was stirring. My seven year old soon awoke, shuffled into the living room and sat on the couch rubbing the sleep and dreams from her eyes. After a few minutes she came over to the desk, pulled up a chair and asked if she could sit next to me. I told her to get a book and we could read together.

So she did and we sat quietly with our feet up on the desk, each reading a book in the peaceful morning hush. I found myself not reading, but watching her as she read. I wondered what created this little, beautiful human being, and marveled at the innocence and purity of the dawn before the day has had a chance to do its damage.

Finally she put her book down and said, "Daddy, when I grow up I want to be a writer."

"Me too," I told her.

Now, before Hallmark swoops in with the idea of using this as a greeting card commercial next Father's Day, I must admit she has also told me recently that, among many other things, she'd like to be the following when she grows up: a teacher, a photographer, a person who sells jewelry and a zookeeper but only for lemurs, toucans and macaws.

I take my victories where I get them nevertheless.

It is so heartwarming when they want to be like me, and yet that is one of my greatest fears. I want them to go into the world and make the right decisions without me there, yet as if I were there.

They are little burrowing earthworms. They don't know that the cool sidewalk of the morning can become a stovetop by midday. When we coax them into the grass, all they feel is a sharp stick in their side and fight back.

And we don't often remember to look at the world through their eyes; to sit quietly and contemplate, to see the wonder and awe all about us.

If we allow ourselves, we have as much to learn from them as they do from us. And maybe that's why we wave at each other on every turn of the merry-go-round.

September 12, 2009

A Store I've Gotten Used To

I CAUGHT the wife in bed with another man last week. I can't really blame her though. It was Hemingway. I mean, who wouldn't? What did freak me out was Steinbeck, Maugham and Fitzgerald stacked up at the foot of the bed waiting for their turn.

It might be time to box up some of these old used books I've collected over the years.

There's just something about a used bookstore I can't resist; the musty, dry fragrance of aging tomes. I imagine the hands that have touched them, absorbed them and passed them on.

There's life in a used bookstore, rooted and time-honoring, that can't be found elsewhere. And for the last 20 years, my sanctuary of the scroll has been Brand Bookshop.

When I tell this to Jerome Joseph, the 81 year old, boyishly energetic owner, he's pointed in his smiling reply: "We've been here for 24 years. Where were you the first four?"

There are local characters who add texture and color to their little corner of our world, none more so than Jerome. A conversation with this book monger is a bumper car ride; you can't really figure out which way the cars are going or how to steer, but you sure enjoy the ride.

Ask him about the store or his childhood and you get back a staccato stream of consciousness en route to his final answer. And almost always the answer has something to do with politics, baseball or his favorite topic, Japan.

From his shop on Brand Boulevard, a former jewelry store, the gems he peddles are used and out-of-print books. And opinions. Opinions on just about everything.

On movies: "I'm tired of American movies. Lot of blood squirting, exploding automobiles and using the F-word every sentence for no purpose."

But he highly recommends "Departures," the Japanese film that won the Academy Award for best foreign language film in 2008. "If you don't like it, I'll refund your rental fee... I'll call you when you can rent it at Video Journeys. As long as I can call you collect."

On Cuba: "The government, I think, is going to end the embargo before too long. Both parties were afraid to lose the vote in Florida, controlled by the anti-Castro Cubans... We talk about not trading with Cuba, but yet we sell them $700 million worth of agricultural goods over the last two years... How hypocritical can you be?"

On Afghanistan: "I think it's a mistake to go in strongly with a surge. Russia had 150,000 troops there, plus 100,000 Afghani troops, and they quit after 10 years. Why do we think we could succeed there?"

On religion: "I'm an agnostic. I'm convinced when you die it's like going to sleep. There's no hereafter." But he adds, "People who are sincerely religious have something that the other person doesn't have. I think they're happier than the one who takes the view that I do."

And most importantly, the designated hitter rule: "I think it's an abomination."

Born near St. Louis, "My father bought me stock in the St. Louis Browns. I used to attend stockholder meetings. Do you remember the time Bill Veeck hired a midget to bat named Eddie Gaedel? I was there that day" — he practiced law in Missouri before moving to California some 50 years ago. After failing the California bar exam three times — "I'd been out of school so long; it's the toughest bar around." He finally gave up on law as a career.

"That's all right, I didn't have the love to practice law."

After some years working in other people's bookstores, he eventually started his own. And in used books he finally found his place.

"I love what I do. My work is my hobby."

Used bookshops are falling victim to higher rents, corporate chains and the ease of Internet shopping. But Jerome attributes his staying power to a shop that is well organized and a staff that is personable and knowledgeable. That and a loyal clientele.

"I wouldn't like a bookstore in a train station where you never see [your customers] again. Here you learn a lot from people."

And what does this frenetic used-book guru read?

"I don't like fiction myself. The time I spend reading, I want to read something that's really happening." That and anything on Japan.

During his brief overseas deployment during the Korean War, he regretted not really seeing Japan. A few years later he returned, and that's when he met his now adopted son, Noriaki Nakano.

Jerome was sitting in a small-town restaurant trying to figure out how to order lunch. A college-aged man sitting at the next table offered help, and a friendship was born.

"He said he'd never met Americans he liked before, and would I mind corresponding with him."

A couple of years later Noriaki came to the U.S. on a student visa and got his master's at Pepperdine.

Noriaki is now the manager of the shop.

"When I die I think he'll sell the place."

Let's hope not.

"I'll quote something for you," Jerome said , sharply turning our bumper car yet again. "The man in charge of the kamikaze corps was Admiral Onishi... Here's his death poem:

'In blossom today, then scattered. Life is so like a delicate flower. How can one expect the fragrance to last forever.'"

But some fragrances do last forever, and you won't find them on the Internet or at the mega-chains. And that's what I can't resist about used bookshops.

January 9, 2010

◦✖◦

Saving the Day, One Snowball at a Time

ALL men yearn to be heroes. But most people are freaked out when a stranger wearing baggy sweat pants, a towel for a cape and boxer briefs on his head for a mask assails them in the supermarket parking lot demanding to carry their groceries. We wannabe heroes need a more captive audience. So we find someone who can keep their breakfast down while looking at us, and we procreate.

The last time I tried to be a hero to my two daughters, to show them a day of outdoor fun they'd never forget, I took them kite flying. Well. . . at least we'll never forget it. The day ended with kids and Dad reduced to tears. The kites are buried in the garage, symbols of repressed childhood memories I fear to unearth.

But last Saturday was simply too beautiful to let pass without another attempt. The nurse-wife was absorbed in her own selfish pastime of caring for sick people and earning a paycheck. Without her guidance, Saturdays are a blank slate upon which I must scribble something if there's to be peace and sanity in the home. So, after four straight days of rain, and seeing the mountains capped with snow like vanilla-frosted chocolate cupcakes, I announce my plan to Thing 1 and Thing 2.

"Let's go to the snow today!"

They scream with delight, and my heart overflows. Then Thing 1 picks up the remote and tells me to get out of the way. SpongeBob just did something funny, and she can't see Squidward's reaction.

"Let's get going. We'll fill up the truck with snow and bring it home!" I say, trying to keep hope alive.

"What? You were serious?" is Thing 1's reply. And when I tell her that I am indeed serious, she melts into a mass of confusion and weeping the likes of which I haven't seen since the first time she saw the Disneyland parade come to an end.

"You can't do that!" she sobs. "You can't just take snow home. Stop saying that!"

Meanwhile, Thing 2 has already put on 14 layers of clothes and the cutest little high-heeled open-toed shoes you've ever seen. Since I really want to do this, I'm going to have to roll the dice and force Thing 1 to go. I swallow my pride and resort to the lowest form of coercion.

"I'll get you McDonald's for lunch on the way home."

"Fine. I'll go," she says. "But I won't like it."

Good enough for me, and we're off. But not before turning back to the house three times. Camera. Nintendo games. Bathroom. So, now that it's past lunchtime, we stop at McDonald's and get three Happy Meals for the drive up. A full mouth stifles whining anyway.

We head up Angeles Crest, and the mountains are spectacular; mounds of new snow just a couple of miles away. But, the sheriff's department had other plans. Roadblock.

"Angeles Crest Highway is closed indefinitely," the kind officer tells me. "Mud and rock slides. Road crews simply haven't had enough time to clear them."

So we, along with 15,000 other families wearing snow gear, stand forlornly outside the barrier like the ticketless outside a Jonas Brothers concert.

"Let's go home," Thing 1 says, a hint of victory in her voice. But, though I know I'm tempting a most unwanted fate, I can't give up now.

"Nothing is over until we decide it is!" I say. "Was it over when the Germans bombed Pearl Harbor?!?" But my rallying cry is lost on them. They fell asleep during the toga party scene the last time we watched "Animal House."

Undaunted, I plot a course for Frasier Park on my iPhone — 68.9 miles north, but I remind the little ones that everything in L.A. is just 20 minutes away. They're young. I can't burst their bubble yet. And before I can get to 25 bottles of beer on the wall, we're seeing snow on the side of the freeway. I exit along with the 15,000 other families and find a place to park next to a bank of untouched powder.

We leap from the car and begin throwing snowballs at each other. But not before I'm reminded that getting gloves onto a child's hands is perhaps the single most frustrating chore in parenting. Like shoving live earthworms into cocktail straws. Soon Things 1 and 2 are happily frolicking in the snow and sun while Daddy shovels several hundred pounds of snow into the truck bed. Thirty minutes later, with frozen toes and wet bottoms, we're back on the road, heater blasting.

The moment we pull into the driveway, neighbor kids come running, and the obligatory snowball fight ensues. There are cries of joy, cries of pain. Dumping snow on the front lawn, I have a vision. With sleds borrowed from the neighbor, and a little civil engineering, the front yard soon resembles the amateur bobsled run at Lake Placid. For the rest of the afternoon we hold Olympic luge trials; schussbooming in Burbank.

"Daddy, you're right," Thing 2 says. "You can bring snow home!"
And my heart grew three sizes.

Hot cocoa and a hot bath end the day. Though we lose a few fingers to frostbite, I sit back and count the day a success.

"Honey, why is there snow on the front lawn?" the wife calmly asks when she comes home.

"Snow day, dear," I tell her proudly.

"And why do you have underwear on your head?"

That one's a little harder to explain.

January 30, 2010

Man Cave's Lament

Warning: No toys were used in the entertainment of these children.

The sun did not shine.
It was too wet to play.
So I cleaned my garage,
Though I'd soon rue the day.

WHEN it's not my "man cave" it's usually one of the following: a beauty salon, cheerleading camp, a kennel for wayward puppies, a high school math class, the Hollywood Bowl or the fanciest restaurant in the world – the Café FruFru.

I am of course referring to my garage, the place of peace for a husband and father. Our very own day spa, where we putter and tinker and idle away time without purpose. It's our filthy little corner of the world and, we hope, a place no one else cares to venture.

But just when I've cleaned it and arranged things exactly how I like, in such a way that fills a man with the kind of inner peace he finds in few other places, my daughters, whom I affectionately and accurately refer to as Thing One and Thing Two, descend upon my fortress of solitude. They're followed shortly thereafter by the kid next door. Then along comes the kid from up the street and a few more from down the street. Then finally a refugee family from Sudan, and I am forced to give up my ground in retreat.

From inside the house I witness as, in $1/100^{th}$ the time it took me to organize my garage, they have transformed it into one of the aforementioned fantasy locations. Dare I so much as glance at them from the kitchen window while they take on the guise of their new personas – cowgirls, teachers and rock stars – and I am screamed at, the demonic intruder breaking down the fourth wall of their collective imagination.

"Dad, don't watch us!" they holler.

I'm forced to wait them out, at my desk I do sit.
I say to myself, "Do I like this? Oh no, not a bit!"

Alas, it won't take long. Like locust with ADD, they soon move on to the living room, the front yard, the neighbor's house, the intersection of Olive and Alameda. And in each new place they create new worlds, oblivious to the people around them, or to the laws of nature or traffic. Yet it mystifies me that they are never able to do this in their own room.

When I return to my temporarily sublet man cave to survey the destruction and take possession of it once again, I'm struck by something odd. It's something I notice every time the locust storm sweeps through and moves on.

No toys.

No toys are ever used in the creation of their imaginary worlds.

An old bookshelf becomes the maitre d's station, my notebooks her reservation list; a furniture pad is a magic carpet floating somewhere over Egypt. Or Silver Lake. Sawhorses become trusted stallions on the open range, chairs are lecture podiums for harsh college professors and planks of scrap wood create a dilapidated bridge over a river of hot lava.

Golf clubs become canes or crutches for the infirm; baseball bats become weapons of mass destruction. Higher and higher up the walls I mount my power tools and anything with a rusty blade. I fear the day they discover the ladder hidden behind their bikes. But if ever there was a safe place to hide something I don't want them to find, it's behind their cobwebbed bikes.

But nary a toy anywhere. Lest you count the jump rope used as a leash to drag a naked Barbie through the dog park or the badminton racket which doubles as a bass guitar. Exactly who the hell is Justin Bieber anyway?

Lemons from the neighbor's tree are mercilessly butchered; their juice, rind and seeds combined in flower pots with birdseed, grass, dirt and leaves from my newly planted basil to create an intoxicating witch's brew. This coven clad in paper clip necklaces, trash bag capes and faces smeared with charcoal, dance around an orange traffic cone, their psychedelic high priestess imbedded in the driveway.

Brooms are still brooms, which is nice. But I just wish they'd actually sweep the dirt, leaves and spilt birdseed out of the garage rather than more deeply into the corners and nooks of it.

"Honey, put the propane tank down gently please!!"

I live in a constant state of panic fearing they will someday realize that my barbecue could easily transform into a spaceship to Mars or a stagecoach across the old west. There's only so much a man can take.

So I picked up all the things that were down
The rake, the axe, the shovel and gown.
Kitchen utensils, oh that's where they went.
It's the flagpole that gave my car a new dent.
With tables and chairs and blankets astray,
Leave it to dad to put all away.

May 1, 2010

Exploring the Adirondacks

I'M always saddened when I see a front porch with no one sitting on it. I notice them most often as I ride my bike through town, or on the rare long walk. You see so much more of the world when you're not in your car.

The overabundance of vacant front porches is made more depressing just before dinner or sunset, times when everyone should stop, sit in front of their house and watch the world go by for a few minutes.

Not long ago I was standing in my front yard watching the daughters do the silly things they do, when I was joined by my neighbor Scott and his daughter. Normally, the girls play in one place for about two minutes before moving on to their next playing field like butterflies with OCD.

But when it appeared they were happy in the front yard, I brought a couple of rarely used, wooden Adirondack chairs from the backyard and set them on the front lawn. Scott and I sat and relaxed.

That night I left those chairs where they were because I'm generally a very lazy person and hate cleaning up after myself. Though I knew they were defenseless against the elements and automatic sprinklers, there was something so pleasing about the sight of them in that corner of the lawn; the Birds of Paradise hedge behind them, the palm trees and neighbor's olive tree providing an arbor overhead.

It's an area the kids hardly explore, making it a perfect place from which to sit and watch them. It's shady and offers a pleasant view of the neighborhood; a great spot from which to yell at the cars speeding down our residential street.

Scott followed his kid down the next day after school, and a bottle of wine magically appeared. The scene repeated itself a few days later. His wife and mine visited, and we found a few more chairs. I dusted off a dilapidated old bamboo end table to set our drinks upon. The chairs are now a fixture on the front lawn. The gardeners move them when they mow, but always place them right back where they belong.

My grandparents were married some 60 years, qualifying them as experts on just about everything in life. They had a name for their evening cocktail: the Shibobby. Legend has it the name was how my oldest sister pronounced the mysterious concoction of Bourbon and water. They liked theirs served tall, in a generic plastic glass. No buckets or tumblers for them.

It was their evening ritual, something these retired folks looked forward to each night. In nice weather we'd sit on their lushly shaded patio as they enjoyed their Shibobby, and we enjoyed their company and their ping-pong table.

When I was a boy playing with my friends around the house, my mother would often call her friend across the street and chat while each made dinner. A parent's diverted attention is a child's invitation to torment.

So we'd use the long cord to the wall-mounted phone as a jump rope, tangling it horribly and preventing any civilized conversation. The following was something my mother said frequently to her friend: "Why don't you just come over for a quick drink?" It was a statement, not a question.

Minutes later the two women would be cackling away over a glass of chardonnay while we kids did everything possible to get their attention. If it was one of "those" days when report cards came home or police were involved, that glass of wine turned into five fingers of Jim Beam. Wild Turkey was poured if the report cards were good or the charges were dropped.

Ever notice how kids lose interest in that thing they simply couldn't live without if it sits in one place too long? The most important toys in the world fade into the background of their ephemeral little lives. But move the Malibu Barbie Beach House just three feet, and it jumps off the screen begging to be played with as if it were brand new. It's kind of like that with those chairs on my front lawn now.

Some mornings I'll be working at my desk and look out the window to see Scott already sitting there with his coffee. I'll grab mine and join him to start our day. Like Fantastic Sam's, there's no appointment needed.

The other evening I saw him approaching with a cheese plate. On cue, I pulled that special bottle of merlot I had chilling in the fridge for just such an occasion. And on "those" days, when I see him approach with a tumbler full of Scotch, I pull my Dewar's from the back of the cupboard, pour myself a sympathetic draw, and join him in the Adirondacks.

Maybe it's the melancholy of summer's impending end, as autumn's tentacles creep in. Or a desire to wrestle the last few nights of warm weather sitting outdoors in the twilight. Maybe it's just a good spot to keep an eye on the kids. Or maybe it's just nice to have a friend to sit and have a Shibobby with as we watch the world go by.

Seasons are changing; time slips away faster than we want. But I think I'll be leaving those chairs on the front lawn a little while longer.

September 25, 2010

Saying Goodbye to a Cold Friend

I KNEW there was trouble when I opened the garage and saw the ominous trail of fluid upon the floor, like blood from a victim's gunshot wound. Something terrible had happened; a sense of dread came over me.

Let's start from the beginning.

Besides the couch that daily withstands the abuses of Thing 1 and Thing 2, a microwave oven and various other household items, my wife and I bought a refrigerator early in our marriage. It was our first joint major appliance purchase.

It solidified a long-term commitment not only to creditors, but also to each other. By buying this together, it says, we promise to live with it and each other for better or worse, for richer or poorer, for breakfast, lunch and dinner.

We're not a high-maintenance couple. Our appliances need not have rolled off a German assembly line and road-tested on the Autobahn. It was a simple refrigerator: white, freezer on top, fridge below, two drawers. No ice maker or water dispenser. Just a fridge.

But it became so much more.

After some years in the kitchen, it was relegated to the garage in our last move, becoming our secondary cold storage. For a family of four, it was nice to have a place for things that would otherwise clutter the in-house icebox. Stocked before backyard parties, it gave visitors easy access to drinks.

On hot days in the pool, it's where you got a cold one so you wouldn't trail water through the kitchen. It was my liquid oasis while working under the hot sun. And that intense sun was, I believe, its demise.

During the scorching September heat wave that recent rains have cast from our memory, I opened my garage to that most unpleasant sight. A blast of sickly hot air washed over me as the garage door rose; a hot box exhaling in relief. But it was too late for the refrigerator baking within that sauna. Wheezing achingly, his life-fluids drained from him.

Yes. It was a him. Where boats, barbecues and hurricanes —
until more metrosexual times — get feminine identities, the garage
fridge can only be male. Why? Because he held everything that
made me feel like a guy. He was my porter; my squat, tough, quiet
Himalayan porter, carrying everything I put on him with dignity,
grace and servitude. Asking only to be plugged in, he held my burdens along with my porterhouse and rib-eye.

He stored meats and steaks, my bounty from hunting trips to
the butcher. Bottles of beer accumulated over time in wide variety. Coke in glass bottles smuggled in by mules from Mexico and
sold at Costco. Butter, not margarine. The White Zinfandel I'm
forced to buy for my sister but won't allow in my house. Wild Koho
salmon caught by my friend Jim in the glacial rivers of Alaska's
backcountry, vacuum-packed and doled out to his lucky neighbors.
Whole chickens — fryers and roasters — three kinds of Italian
sausage and two boxes of those fish sticks with the ruddy, depend-
able fisherman on the logo. I even had buffalo ribs in there.

All gone.

His presence in my garage is something I took for granted. We
do that to our loved ones; their consistency in the background of
our lives makes us complacent. I knew he was always there for me.
Each time I opened the garage, he had something to offer: beer, red
meat and dependability. And now... and now he's gone, and I'm
left with this phantom urge.

I made chili the other day, and chili must be made in quantity.
Feed half to my family tonight, and store half in the garage freezer
for a cold winter's night. I got to the back door before the realiza-
tion set in. It was a heavy feeling in my gut the size of a tri-tip roast.

"He's gone," the wife said sympathetically to my back. I couldn't
turn to face her. Sure, I could squeeze it into the kitchen freezer
next to the dumplings, frozen peas and bagel bites. But it's just not
the same.

When I found him in that condition that horrible day, I
attempted resuscitation. Unplugged him and plugged him back in
repeatedly, hoping for a jolt of defibrillation. Cleaned the grates.
Turned the knobs from "cold" to "coldest" and back again over
and over.

Nothing.

My garage fridge is dead.

A while back I hung a bottle opener on a string right next to him for convenience. It's a bottle opener I purloined from a bar in the Andes while en route to the Inca Trail with the woman who would become my wife. He loved that story.

I took the bottle opener down, put it in a drawer and walked out of the garage, leaving him unplugged.

Adios, amigo. You will be missed.

October 23, 2010

A Trip to Hollyweird

KEEPING the kids entertained is a parent's primary job. It ranks higher than feeding and cleanliness. In the throes of a good time, hunger and head lice are but minor annoyances.

With a free day, where could the wife and I take the kids without passports, plane tickets or extended lines of credit?

Hollywood.

At least we wouldn't need passports or plane tickets.

A day trip to the entertainment capital of the world is a perfect way to kill a few hours so long as we return with both girls. To better those odds, we take along one of their friends. Travelling with a friend also keeps them focused on each other rather than how bored they are.

Stemming more from my hatred of parking structures than civic or global responsibility, we take public transportation rather than drive ourselves or hire a private helicopter. This gives our excursion a gritty realism rarely found on family vacations.

Deep in the bowels of the Earth under Universal City, we stand on the platform waiting for the Metro Red Line. Thing 1 and Thing 2 move nervously about, avoiding eye contact with strangers while appreciating the artistic tile work and pungent aromas. Their friend, Thing 2.5, sits on the dusty floor scribbling in her autograph book. Or maybe she's taking notes to report back to her parents:

Day One of my captivity with the Canedays. Female parent seems nice, but male emits foul odor and appears deaf. Will remain obedient until he's had his evening cocktail. Hunger beginning to set in.

Feeling the telltale rushing wind of the approaching train, I tell the girls to stop playing on the tracks.

"Mind the gap!" I holler in my deepest British tenor.

The male parent pleases himself in making obscure references unintelligible to children.

Though it's only an eight-minute ride through a dark tunnel from the valley to Hollywood, the Red Line is more accurately an eight-minute trip through a wormhole from sanity to psychedelic. I forget how popular Hollywood is, with sightseers from around the world. Riding the escalator up into the midday sun of Hollywood Boulevard I feel like Richard Dreyfuss boarding the spaceship at the end of "Close Encounters of the Third Kind."

The touristy scene is reminiscent of those in front of the Leaning Tower of Pisa, the Eiffel Tower or Buckingham Palace, though I doubt you'd see Spiderman, Yoda and Michael Jackson taking pictures with tourists in front of those landmarks. Thousands of people with cameras, fanny packs, sandals and socks, bump into one another, all staring down at the stars on the ground.

"Look girls! Lon Chaney!" I screech in schoolgirl excitement.

I'm baffled at how my counterparts live under these conditions...

When you do look up, you're face to face with one of the 1,583 tour wranglers trying to get you onto a converted, roofless Ford Econoline van that will show you what may or may not be the gates and driveways of the rich and famous.

Walking with seven and eight year olds is an exercise in evasive reflexes under normal circumstances. But trying to keep them in single file on a busy sidewalk is a unique torture and test of patience. So we make frequent stops in the souvenir shops. Here we only need to keep them from handling the palm tree snow globes.

Thing 1 spies a stuffed toy poodle in Gucci handbag, a la Paris Hilton. Thing 2 finds a mock parking sign: "Stoner Parking Only — Violators will be... ah, whatever, dude." And Thing 2.5 wants the life-size George Clooney cardboard standee.

The wife makes final decisions on all souvenir purchases: "No on the poodle. No on the sign. Yes on George. But I'll hold him for you."

We bypass the wax museums and Believe-It-or-Not Odditorium in favor of avoiding bankruptcy. And we forgo the Guinness World of Records when I discover it has nothing to do with drinking ale.

The real attraction isn't the Walk of Fame, cement footprints or costumed out-of-work actors letting strangers photograph them wearing spandex for tips. No, the real scene is the people on the streets — the angry, Black Panther-like mob videotaping itself in protest against The Man, Big Business and organized religion; the singing band of wandering born-again Christians handing out leaflets with a smile, preaching the love of God while holding a sign depicting tourists burning in hell; the earnest, welcoming Scientologists offering free stress tests.

A group of out-of-towners is mesmerized by their siren song. I grab the probes of a stress-measuring machine, and it shorts out in a spray of sparks.

"Run!" I yell, and they flee, woken from a dream.

As we head back to the subway, I pause dreamily on Charlize Theron's star.

"Daddy!" Thing 1 yells impatiently, and I snap back to reality.

"Hey, girls! Look! Don Haggerty!"

Will escape on subway, fend for myself. Pray for me.

November 20, 2010

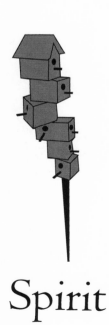

Spirit

When you walk to the edge
Of all the light you have
And take that first step into the darkness
Of the unknown,
Faith is knowing
One of two things will happen:
There will be something solid for you to stand upon
Or, you will be taught to fly

~Patrick Overton

What shall it profit a man if he gains the whole world
but loses his soul?

~ Jesus Christ

Ascending

THERE is a bluff overlooking a vast lava field somewhere in New Mexico. A spectacular floe of ebony shards where the cliffs are islands in a molten sea silently stretching away from you with the curve of the earth.

And it pains me that I will probably never in my life be able to find that exact spot again. I could search for it; maybe find a similar vista over some natural wonder, but never that specific bluff again. Frankly, it was so long ago I wouldn't know where to start, wouldn't know that precise location if I were standing on it. And this saddens me because it was on that mesa that I felt closer to God then I had ever felt before. Or since.

I was about twenty-five years old and driving solo through the Southwest. I used to travel like this whenever I got the chance; just me and my truck loaded with camping gear, books, food, music and wine. No schedule, just drive as long or as short as you felt like each day. When you see something of interest, pull over and check it out. So when I saw a sign directing travelers to a lava field in the middle of the otherwise barren desert, I knew it was something I shouldn't miss.

There were no other people around. Not a soul. And that always makes me wonder about humanity. Shouldn't there be a line here? Doesn't a place like this warrant more interest than a Lady Gaga YouTube video?

These were pre-iPod times, so I grabbed my portable tape deck, walked out upon the cliffs and found a nice place to sit and gaze over the endless expanse of lava. It was silent; a still ocean of black rocks frozen in mid squall. So I sat in the stillness with the winds nudging me from all directions, just trying to take it all in. There is a forced meditation in a place like this, a hush and reverence one can't help but obey. I felt a similar awe the first time I approached the Grand Canyon. Upon coming through the trees and seeing that cavernous, surreal hole, silent wonder is the only respect to be paid.

I don't know how long I was there before I was finally joined by another visitor. A bird. I'd like to say it was a hawk or an eagle. Or a falcon. But I'm no bird watcher, so I have no idea what it was. It was big, though, with broad, long outstretched wings. And it was majestic.

I watched as this solitary creature rose and descended before me, riding invisible thermals over the dusty land and obsidian sea. With the subtlest movement of its wingtips, it gently lifted and sank in lazy spirals; reaching a pinnacle only to drop down and start over time and again, undisturbed by the world or gravity's effort to end its journey.

On my Walkman a collection of random classical music was playing. "The Lark Ascending" by Vaughan Williams came on, and it fit this moment like the mystery ingredient that brings a seven-course meal together. Or the key that unlocks a mysterious steamer trunk that's been hidden away in your attic for years.

The violins and flute of this pastoral arrangement, the wings and wind, play with each other, rising to crescendos and falling to valleys, one buoying the other, up and down. The strings flutter, the winds gently lift them to new heights, over and over and over, until the sun crawled below the horizon to rest.

It was in this moment, watching a bird sail over the desert, that I truly understood what worship was. I wasn't a churchgoer at the time, but I knew that I was in the presence of something greater than me, something that had a plan, something that wanted my attention and was trying to get it by being subtle. I was in the midst of something that wanted me to appreciate not only this place and time, this bird, these winds and notes, but also appreciate its existence through them. It wasn't begging me to adore it in some ego-filling way; wasn't looking to be praised and fawned over. It simply said, "Look. See what I've done for you," in the most generous and gracious way possible with no ulterior motive; a sadness, a hope and joy in its speechless voice all at the same time.

This place, this earth, these sights and sounds, are a cathedral like none ever created with human hands. I knew then I was in the presence of my maker, an awesome and mysterious God who knows so much more than we do, and speaks in wordless languages that can only be heard when stillness reigns, when we shut out the clamoring voices and distractions around us.

I didn't discover God that day. And it would be some time before I started actually attending church. I wasn't done being self-absorbed just yet; wasn't done flitting around like a daydreaming, beer-swilling butterfly. I don't know that I've ever totally gotten over that.

No. What happened that day was more re-acquaintance; tapping into something I already knew, already felt. And now I understood it just a little bit better because it spoke to me directly for the first time, not through someone else's words and interpretation, but in a language I could understand that was just between us.

I've heard a lot of people give their testimony, stand up before a group and tell them the why, how and when of their particular journey toward healing and salvation. I've heard about near death experiences, all-consuming addictions to pornography, drugs and alcohol; about abandonment, abusive parents and spouses. I've heard war stories; of frightened, angry men looking down the barrel of a gun at another human a hair trigger away from taking their life. And of being the one in that shooter's crosshairs.

Most of the time these orations take place in church or a church-like setting, and are meant to offer encouragement and support to those in attendance. They are ways of sharing one's battles so others may realize they aren't alone; an average person preaching to a choir of listeners who share his or her belief. They can be powerful moments demonstrating just how long God's reach is and his ability to raise even the most self-loathing and degenerate.

I've always shied away from giving my testimony in these settings, never raised my hand to offer it. When the pastor asks for volunteers, I find it a convenient time to go to the restroom. There are two reasons for this. One is my lifelong fear of speaking in public. My throat seizes, my head goes foggy and my mouth turns to cotton. The other reason is that I don't believe I have a testimony, or at least not one as interesting or valuable as everyone else's. I have nothing worthy to offer those who might need a reason to go to church or even continue going.

But when I look back and think about the day on that bluff overlooking the lava fields, and so many days before and since, I guess I do have a story; just not a made-for-TV movie one like so many others I've heard.

I hate to call it a "testimony" though. That makes it sound so "churchy." Church-speak is a language I've never been particularly comfortable with. To the outsider it sounds silly, put on and practiced; too many puppy-dog looks and "amens" and "blessings" and wistful interjections about the love of God as if it were a milk crate full of kittens; dreamy-eyed recountings of God's grace in answering prayers for a great parking place at the crowded mall during the Christmas rush.

Thankfully, I've come to find that God is an artist who works in mosaic. Though he's constant and unchanging, he has as many personalities as he has creations. One of them pulls a seat up next to me at the bar, orders a beer and listens while I pour out my sorrows. He isn't offended when I get mad and lash out at him irrationally, but takes it like a good friend does. Another tries to get my attention by saying silly things to me in the bothersome voice of a four-year-old child while I'm trying to meet my deadline or come up with the perfect witticism to post on Facebook. And yet another is a stranger, the one I overhear while standing in line for coffee, or behind me on the elevator talking about their crazy ex or their great new job, that reminds me there are others out there more pitiful or more graceful than me.

I've seen the face of God that's bigger than the restrictions we put on him, because even he told us that he's too vast for us to comprehend. I know the one that's big enough to have a unique voice for each of his unique children. I know the one that speaks to us as if we're alone in the desert and searching for something we have no idea how to find. That's when he sends a bird, a song and a breeze. Or, as he most often does, a person.

My older sister was a child of the 70s, for all its earnest rock opera, bell bottoms, long hair and rebellion. She was living the life, and her rotation of groovy, disheveled vagabond associates reflected the times. Most of them came and went. But one day she brought Jesus home — and she never let him leave.

She began living the godly life with an even greater zeal then she had her rebellious life. Jesus was her intoxication now and she was passing that pipe around to friends and family with the intensity and stubbornness that defined her. And I was a good younger brother who did what he was told. So I took the pipe. I was twelve and she was seven years my senior. She was wiser than I was, of course. Still is. And I trusted her. Frankly, I was just glad she was speaking to me, which was uncommon before her conversion. Until then she was brooding and remote. But now she was actually involving me in her life, smiling at me, with me and for me. Of course whatever she said about Jesus was right. Just look what he'd done with her!

I was a shy kid. Not given to making friends easily and always seeking the acceptance and approval of others in order to feel better about myself. And this invitation to God's party gave me the smallest feelings of inclusion. So I took a big hit of God, and held it in for a long time.

I spent my teenage years keeping my beliefs mostly private though. I'd been stung by schoolyard taunts on the occasions that I did open up and feared doing anything that would make me appear different from anyone else. The still small voice inside my heart got stiller and smaller until I became just another average kid. In high school, I discovered a marvelous anesthetic for teenage awkwardness: beer. With its help, I was able to make new friends, feel comfortable around strangers and fit in. Partying became the acceptable way to define yourself, a tent pole to gather round no matter how different you each were. The disenfranchised could get just a few steps closer to the campfire if they brought beer and wine coolers. And it was nice to feel welcome somewhere finally.

Drinking to fit in, to feel brave and comfortable, took me through high school and into college. By then it simply became a part of life — at the student union after class, at clubs, at parties. I never stopped believing in God; occasionally when faced with the decision to do something right or wrong, I'd hear him talking to me. But that belief went dormant, stuffed down under the much better feeling of acceptance among one's peers. Or stuffed down under beers if I wanted to do something the still small voice told me I shouldn't.

After college, I found a job that afforded me a meager living. It was the 1990s, a great time for those that liked the metaphysical more than the heavy metal. The New Age movement was sweeping the land. People were dusting off their Edgar Cayce and Shirley MacLaine books. Anyone with a past life regression story of healing and acceptance and harmony could write a best seller telling you how to embrace the light. The mystic music of Yanni and Enya were the background score for those seeking enlightenment; no one was turned away. All were welcome.

I visited ashrams, burned incense, attended the séances of renowned spiritual advisors with direct links to souls on the other side. I would sit up all night with a couple bottles of cheap merlot listening to an angry, poetic Tori Amos or synthetically evocative Tangerine Dream and read Rumi or Emerson, the Tao Te Ching or the Baghavad Gita, until I discovered the secrets of life itself.

A new world had opened to me. I finally felt comfortable talking about things spiritual. Religion was too restrictive and old fashioned though; too many rules created by men. This new spirituality was the universe that encompassed everything harmoniously within it, including religion. But in this new spirituality, divinity was within you, and therefore you created your own reality. Self-expression, self-discovery and self-fulfillment were the rule of the day. There was no wrong path.

But the problem with this kind of thinking, I eventually came to believe, is that humans aren't perfect. We tend to make mistakes and do damage to ourselves and others. If divinity was within us, mankind could never live up to that responsibility. In short, we let ourselves down, when a benevolent, all-knowing, all-loving God can't. No matter how far away he seems at times.

Somewhere during my aimless spiritual meanderings, God sent another person to me; a woman who was not repulsed by my awkwardness and mental flights of fancy. Like no one else, she had the magical, calming ability to make me feel welcome not only in her embrace, but in my own skin. And against her better judgment, she agreed to marry me.

We were soon joined by two daughters. Two, beautiful, amazing, little beings that prove miracles can happen.

I've never battled a serious life threatening illness or injury. Outside that, I can think of few things that reduce a person to their pure, raw, vulnerable human state more than a six-month-old child that will not let you sleep more than two hours in a row. For six months in a row. This, combined with the dawning knowledge that you are now ultimately responsible for another human being, has a destructive effect upon one's sanity.

Though you set out with good intentions to be the best parent ever, to avoid with militant watchfulness the mistakes you believe your parents made, you find yourself making completely new and fantastic mistakes. You fail and get angry and wonder what you did in some past life to warrant such punishment in this one. In your calmer moments, when the kids are fed and sleeping, you agonize over how they'll ever get through life functionally with you as their parent.

The answer, I would come to realize, was not within me.

I think it's one of God's great inside jokes that he uses children to bring people to him. It's diabolical actually. Just when you think you've got life all figured out, you're given children. And the frustration, sleeplessness, anger and self-doubt that accompanies them. You find yourself reaching out to others more than you ever had before, seeking outside help in remaining sane and finding answers. I think it's God's way of getting our attention. It's his way of reminding us that, as your children are to you, you are to him.

So one Sunday we tried it. It being church. "Just to see" what it was like. "Just to see" if we could find some solace or peace or confirmation that we were in fact not going completely mad.

And what we found were people willing and happy to watch our crying children for 90 minutes while we listened to someone talk about the long road to peace. What we found were still more people sitting next us who were suffering similarly or even worse.

And that is why we went back the following Sunday, and most Sundays since.

I can't sing, I have no musical talent. But over the years my voice has risen from silent lip synching to a comfortable, unashamed voice among the others. Sometimes I don't sing, but close my eyes and listen to all of the other voices lifted up around me in praise, surrounding me, spiraling up to the rafters. When my faith is weak, I'm buoyed on the faith of others.

We don't sing traditional hymns. We sing modern songs. I don't lift my hands up in uncontrolled praise like so many others do, trying to get just that much closer to God when the spirit calls them. The spirit moves me also, but for some reason I keep my hands down. I do like to see others though, reaching out to touch him. That makes my heart happy.

We take communion once a month. We all get our cracker and hold it until everyone has been served. Then we eat it together. I like to place the cracker in my mouth, then wait, and listen to 200 misfits, crooks, thieves, idolaters, unstable parents and suffering children crunch in unison. "We believe. Thank you," is lifted up to the heavens.

And this is why I feel safer at church than anywhere else. Church is filled with people who have finally admitted that we can't endure the madhouse alone. We are lost, scared, and unsure, even if it doesn't look that way on the outside; despite our words and arrogance and sureness.

I may disagree with people in my church and in the greater body throughout the world. I don't always like what they say or how they say it. No message of love and peace is ever received when it's delivered with venom, hatred and condescension. There are things I understand, and things I don't. There are things I do understand, but wish I didn't have to. Because I am human. And I am challenged by faith.

I curse. I enjoy good Scotch and Tequila, sometimes more than I should. While channel-surfing the other night, I stalled just a little too long on "Spring Break Bikini Adventures."

Though I know I'm not supposed to, I often drive my children to wrath. But the little Pharisees had it coming.

I don't watch Fox News, and I don't think Sarah Palin walks on water. I don't even think she walks on earth. I think tea parties are for extinct colonists and my seven-year-old daughter. I don't care if two men or two women want to marry each other, and if they could, it would have no bearing on the sanctity of my marriage. My scorecard in converting atheists, pagans and liberals to my religion is empty; I love sinners and don't really care about their sin; and whenever someone at church calls to see if I can help serve the children, serve the community or serve the poor, I find I'm too busy serving myself.

I don't fight the culture wars to force others to live under God.

If I could just change my job, my service to the church, my TV viewing habits; If I could just change my desires, my political persuasion and so many other things about me, then I'd figure this all out. I'm just having such a hard time doing that, and I don't know why.

It's not that I don't want to be a better follower, or don't take steps to be more "Christ-like." I want to get closer to God.

But I'm handed this gnawing, guilty feeling that I don't serve God up to some standardized score; that I haven't done enough for him or under him.

Though I've never been arrested for blocking the entrance to an abortion clinic, I feel like I'm in jail; the prison of being a challenged Christian. I feel like Paul in Rome, chained to a jail cell wall, beaten and bloodied, unable to break out and do all of the things I'm told I need to do for God. All Paul could do was pray; all he could do was sing in his cell. Because when he did that, when he found some pithy little way to have communion with his God, the earth shook and the walls fell and the cell doors flew open. That's when Paul got his chance to escape. That's when Paul could run free and continue serving God, for him and under him.

But he didn't.

He stayed.

Given the clear sign to run, he stayed in his circumstances.

I work. I write and try to find ways to provide for my family. When I am home I try to contribute by cooking and cleaning. I do their dishes and their laundry whenever I can. I drop the kids off at school and pick them up, then help them with their homework. I talk to my wife and rub her feet after she's had a long day as a nurse, or an even longer day as a mother. As much as possible I sit in front of my computer and try to find something meaningful to say to people in written words. When I have spare time, I take a bike ride. Those are my circumstances. Lonely, self-absorbed things like that.

Nothing sacred.

Maybe the best I can do is sing; sing while I fold clothes or stand over the stove. Maybe the best I can do is pray as I ride my bike. Maybe the best I can do is find some way to be *with* God while I do my selfish chores, since I'm obviously incapable of doing anything else for him, under him or in service to him.

And I hope that's good enough for God; being with me. Because that's his name. Emmanuel. God with us.

Faith is the long timeless knowing of rainwater that it can destroy mountains and carve vast canyons. Faith is the line we draw from ourselves to that thing out there in the distance we can barely make out through the fog and haze and pollution; and in that thing we know there is peace and resolution. Faith is the bridge upon which we walk when we can't see what's on the other side. Below the bridge is a chasm of confusion and despair and madness. Behind us are regrets. And on the other side, we know, is something better than where we are now.

Whether that bridge is made of frayed rope and decaying wooden planks over a glacial crevasse, or concrete and steel spanning great expanses of ocean, it is the same. Unique to the one who crosses it. It can be bold, defiant and self-righteous. But it is at its best when it is patient, humble and enduring. That is faith in its truest form.

Strip away the politics, the pundits, the finances and scandals. Shut up the voices inside your head, on your radio and television, and even from your pulpit. What you are left with is yourself. A wretch. Flawed, frail, damaged, faulty and misguided. Imperfect.

Having made mistakes, hurt people as well as yourself. And grace, amazing grace, in one breath is both the admission of that and acceptance of help from the deepest part of our soul. When sung, it comes from the lowest part of our being and rises up over and over and over in glorious rapture to the final understanding that we are not in control. We have failed and will continue to fail. But we are loved and accepted despite ourselves.

At faith all arguments inevitably cease. Whether the line you draw is from you to an unseen deity or a mathematical equation; a bridge from earth to heaven. Everything ends in faith. There the bell rings and the fighters go back to their corners, both believing the decision will go their way.

The response to our faith is grace. Amazing grace. It's more than a hymn. To the faithful it is a theme song, a rallying cry. A reward. It may come when you are halfway across the bridge. It may come before you've even started the journey. It may come when you reach the other side. But it always shows up, and rarely in the form you wanted or expected.

A blind and willing faith is, I think, a requirement to any belief. If its reward is grace, then its curse is trial. Faith will be tested. Mine is every day. I doubt. I question. I wonder. And I just don't know. But my belief that there is a God, a creator, a benevolent and all-knowing being, is resolute. In my mind it takes more faith to believe that our existence is an accidental collision of molecules in an ancient cosmic soup and that we are the masters of our own destiny than it does to believe in a designer that is intelligent. There had to be a chef for that soup, right?

There's something beyond description about faith that no person will ever be able to fully explain. Even to those who have shared it, it makes its presence known in myriad ways. That is where I find some sense of peace, in those indescribable places and moments where all I have to cling to is that incomprehensible mystery that is faith.

There are so many bluffs in this world, times in our lives when we feel close to our maker or that spirit we try to describe in words but fail. They are all different, never the same, and that's the point.

We can't capture it like lightning in a bottle. But seeking that close-ness to our maker is the lifelong journey, the eternal struggle of our souls. It's what we were made for.

I'm not old, but I'm not young either. And with each year I find that I know less than I did the previous year. But I know this without the least doubt: we are all seeking something of a higher call. Whether we seek it at the top of a mountain, the depths of the ocean, in a monastery or a shopping mall, we are all trying to fill some yawning emptiness deep within our souls.

Some slake this thirst by fasting or taking drugs, others by run-ning marathons or buying the next digital music player, video game box or shiny new luxury car. Others put pen to paper in an effort to exorcise the voices inside that will not, cannot, be silenced until that thought is made real outside their minds. And others yet make musical instruments sing with such precision and beauty that they know they have just taken one more step away from the rest of us and one step closer to God.

I'll never find that cliff-top again. Something tells me I'm not meant to. But I may find something more on a beach at sunset or a desert road at sunrise; in the pews or on a mountain trail; pick-ing up my kids from school, watching over them as they sleep or making s'mores with them by a roaring campfire; maybe on a run or bike ride, sitting next to my wife watching TV or trash-talking with good friends at the poker table. Each is a gift.

I'm still on my desert road trip, still looking out over a vast, scarred world and trying to find some meaning. I'm on my own road to Damascus, looking for that spot, that place where I hear God's voice speaking to me, and only me.

Not the Best at Praying, But I Do It

I PRAY.

There, I said it. I pray. I am not a good pray-er by any means. In fact, I am rather bad at it.

No, I am not going to rally City Hall to make your kids take five minutes each day to pray in school; nor am I going to knock on your door and ask if you'd like to come to church with me. I am not here to write another column about faith and God. I am here to shine a bright, unflattering dentist light on myself in hopes that you may read this and think, "Thank God I am not as naïve/vain/shallow/misguided (pick the adjective that best applies) as that guy." It is a public service and you are welcome.

My most frequent place of prayer is in the car as I pull out of the driveway and head to work five days a week. That prayer, chanted in a whimpering, small voice, is rather pathetic and usually goes something like this:

"Please, please, please help me today. Oh, please, please, please, please help me."

After I repeat that about 10 times, I may veer into something like this:

"Please help me not to scream (too loudly) at my co-workers, wife, children or the strangers that may wander into my airspace today. Please hold my tongue and keep me patient and calm during the very frustrating things I know will come my way today even though it would feel so much better to just explode in a venomous rage. Please keep me from going insane or having a psychotic episode today. Oh, please, please, please, please help me."

I told you it was pathetic.

Unfortunately, I only have a five-minute commute, so this is about all that gets squeezed in.

Every once in a while, but not often enough, I pray for other people: friends, family, co-workers, Britney Spears.

If you know me and you are reading this right now, yes, I have probably prayed for you once or twice. If you were getting married or divorced, having a new baby or trouble with your teenager, moving to a great new job or getting laid off, I probably prayed for you.

Don't get all warm and fuzzy though. When I pray for others it is usually because I hit a red light and can't think of anything else about myself to talk about.

There is a story that I love, a parable if you will.

A man sits in a bar telling the bartender how he crashed his plane in the remote frozen tundra and thought he was forsaken. He called out to God and waited in vain for divine intervention that never came.

When the bartender asks how he finally got out, the disgruntled man tells him that some stupid Eskimo eventually came by and helped him.

Churchgoer or not, most everyone can associate with that guy wallowing in the frozen wastelands. We all know what it's like to be desperate and needy and angry when we don't get what we want or expect. But why is it no one ever says, "Yeah, I know how that Eskimo felt?"

One day before work recently I took a bike ride, and as I was returning home down the side streets between the Chandler Bikeway and my house, I saw a man digging through someone's recycling bin on the street. It was trash day, and he was gathering cans and bottles to take to the recycling center for cash when a gentleman came out of a nearby house and began hollering at him to go away. I half expected him to throw rocks at the guy as if he were a pesky raccoon in the backyard.

Now, I rarely ever speak up in situations like this. All too often I keep my mouth shut and fume about it later thinking of all the things I should have said. When I do speak up, it is usually a stammering, messy, emotional, caffeine-fueled splattering of random nouns, verbs, conjunctions and exclamations, leaving people wide-eyed and agog in confusion. I am better on paper than in person. Trust me.

But in my mind, I am a cross between Indiana Jones, Abraham Lincoln, Gandhi and Brad Pitt's character in "12 Monkeys." In my mind I turned around and tore in to that gentleman with a biting soliloquy so profound it would make Shakespeare blush and Bill O'Reilly prostrate himself before me. It would have begun with something about "a man not good enough to go through your trash, eh?" And ended with something like, "I knew Mother Teresa. Mother Teresa was a friend of mine. And you sir, are no Mother Teresa." But, in reality had I actually said something, had I stopped and let my feelings vomit forth right there on the street, what I probably would have said was:

"Be the Eskimo!"

January 3, 2009

❧

My BFF is Better than Your BFF

IS IT just me or is work a woeful misery for everyone lately?

With the state of the world right now it feels as if a cloud of doom is hovering over the work week. Budget cuts mean doing the same job with fewer resources. Co-workers who have become friends are moving on to new jobs. Good people are getting laid off, fueling anxiety over the next layoff. I am afraid of taking any phone call for fear of more problems or bad news. But I'm glad I picked up one particular call recently.

The day started off bad. I got into an argument with my five year old over how many scoops of strawberry powder she was allowed to put into her morning milk. I won the argument, and she had a tantrum. Victory is not so sweet after all.

On my drive to work I prayed my daily prayer. You know the one: Please, please, please, please help me today. It's more of a supplication than a prayer, I guess. If there was a way to drive while prostrated, begging for miraculous intervention, I would.

Once at work things didn't get any better. With recent staffing reductions, it means more work and responsibility for those of us left behind. I guess that's a good thing. Job security they call it. I call it depressing.

While in the midst of a crisis that I can't even remember now, my cell phone rang. It was my BFF. Let's call him BiFF. BiFF and I met on the first day of kindergarten. He vividly remembers the exact moment on the monkey bars. Me? Not so much. But he's never held that against me.

At 13 we swore to each other we would be each other's best man when we got married. Thankfully we both found wonderful, charitable women — with obviously questionable judgment in men — that would actually marry us so we could make good on our teen-age pact.

BiFF had just finished a meeting near my office and was standing outside on the street wondering if I was free for a quick coffee. No, I wasn't. But I went anyway.

There are four Starbucks shops within walking distance of my office, but we walked across the street to Priscilla's Coffee. It's warm and personal there — a great neighborhood spot. The people are friendly, the coffee beans aren't over-roasted and every drink is a double shot. It's the kind of place that makes it easy for two old friends to get off the carousel and catch their breath. Friendships can't be franchised.

BiFF is the kind of guy who can carry just about any conversation. He's naturally warm and forthcoming and happy to speak to any topic, but not in that annoying, self-centered way like some of your other friends. Me, for instance. He attempted to tell me about his meeting, his day, idle chit-chat, but I was too obsessed with my own gloom. The hallmark of any great conversationalist is their ability to listen. And that day BiFF did just that.

He listened to me complain and mope, going on about work and my own private hell. Then he did what all good friends do. He did not try to solve my problems. He merely offered up encouraging support, promised that things would get better and reminded me that at least I still had a job, food on the table, a roof over my head, and look at my home life — my amazing wife and beautiful, happy children — and the fact that I get to spill my guts in print each week, serving up my angst and vitriol to potentially dozens of readers all across Burbank. That made me feel a little better.

I am normally a pretty positive person, but BiFF takes optimism to new heights. He has a zest for life I've always admired, an energy that drives him to achieve the often wild ideas he dreams up. He has an exuberance and conviction that is a truly uncommon gift. He does not always achieve his goals but that is not as important to him as trying. Without dreams, we have nothing.

He also has the greatest memory of any person I have ever met. Besides the fact that he remembers in detail the moment we first met, he often relays stories about other old acquaintances.

"Hey, guess who I ran into the other day. Joey Bagadonuts. Remember him?" he'll say.

Long pause on my part. "Nope."

"Sure you do! Joey Bagadonuts, third grade, sat in the fourth row on the left side near the sink 'cuz he threw up that one time during a slide show on sea cucumbers. Hairy arms, smelled like vapor rub, wore red Keds."

Longer pause. "Yeah, no."

"Huh. Funny. He doesn't remember you either. But he said to say hi."

Later that day after work, I got this e-mail from BiFF: "Hugs and laughs!!! Stress less, my friend. It will all work out the way it is intended to. You'll make the right things happen when the time is right. I have faith in you, and more importantly so does your family."

He picked me up, dusted me off and placed me back on the merry-go-round, just a little more prepared for all that the day would bring.

I've said it before and I'll say it again, because it always surprises me and deserves repeating. God works through people. He's been working through BiFF for the last 36 years. And it's so comforting to have a BFF remember you once in a while.

March 14, 2009

Flying Kites on a Cloudy Day

I CAN do pony tails, but my braids are painful and sloppy.

I have two daughters whom I love and adore more than it is possible to describe. Sometimes I can pass as a parent. Sometimes my efforts are like my braids.

The day started like any other Sunday. Wake up, watch TV, Fruity Pebbles, cartoons.

"What are we going to do today?" they ask.

"Go to church," I respond.

Whine, complain, relent. Get dressed, change clothes, brush teeth. Change clothes. Change clothes. Change clothes.

It was a blustery day. Cloudy, slight drizzles, windy. The sermon came from a section of the Bible commonly referred to as the "Hall of Faith," wherein every sentence begins with "By faith..." and goes on to describe the amazing things a procession of biblical figures did by simply living through faith. In other words, people that threw off the Bell Curve for the rest of us.

The topic was Moses' parents and how their faith in just the first few months of his life established a stronghold in him. The Bible is a little fuzzy about what else this guy Moses did with the rest of his life.

The clouds blew away that afternoon, and the sky was blue as blue can be. With a good breeze going, it was the perfect day to fly a kite. The girls were overjoyed at the thought. They usually are when the day takes them to Toys R Us. We packed up a cooler full of drinks and snacks and set out with visions of this being one of those moments in a family's life that would be a benchmark for happiness. Years later they would recall it with rapturous joy, thanking me in their acceptance speech for the Nobel Prize in Aerodynamics... "it all started that day our father took us to fly a kite..."

We bought our kites — Tinkerbell, an owl and a WWII Fighter Plane. Guess which was mine — and went to the wide open field at a local park. They played on the jungle gym while I assembled the kites. As usually happens when a boy tackles a project to build or destroy something, I was engrossed. So much so that I paid no attention to the clouds moving in. Looking back now, they moved in a direction I've never seen clouds move, as if they had a purpose.

The Tinkerbell kite was built and off went the five year old, running and screaming with delight. Exactly the scene I pictured. I assembled the owl and off went the seven year old, equally happy. It was all coming together. A parent's dream: happy children playing outdoors in perfect harmony.

Now I could focus on my fighter plane, an intricate craft requiring much attention to detail. Out of the corner of my eye I could see the girls' kites soaring and falling, soaring and falling. I interrupted my kite building several times to get them back in the air. The magic of this moment was slowly draining from their eyes, the way it does when kids realize something is not as easy as it looks on TV. Perseverance is a trait that comes later in life. At least that's something my mother told me recently.

Just as I was finishing my kite, eager for takeoff, I felt the first drop of rain and willed myself to ignore it. This was difficult because my mind was equally occupied trying to ignore the fact that the temperature had dropped to near freezing.

Right when I launched my kite, first one daughter then the other came sulking back asking to go home. With hands full on my own kite, I tried to delay them. "Keep running. It'll get your kite back in the air and warm you up."

But it was too late. They were done and there would be no convincing them otherwise. Their cries increased. My kite had just taken wing, a streak of blue fighting back an angry sky. The wind picked up, as did the crying. Kites, streamers and string were everywhere. Tinkerbell was grounded and tangled. The wise old owl was silent. But I was not done.

I snapped. "Can't you just try to have a good time?"Rhetorical questions are lost on little ones.

"I want to go home," was the self-pitying refrain.

Frustrated and enraged, I commanded them to sit down and be quiet. But my voice wasn't mine. It sounded like my father's in the rare moments I'd heard him angry. And it scared me.

I looked to the sky for peace and assistance but only saw my fighter plane crash to the ground.

As I stuffed everything into the cooler, including the kites and my sunglasses, I got in one last shot. "All we try to do is show you guys a good time. Try to keep you entertained and make you happy. I guess all you want to do is stay home and watch TV."

And there was a silence so thick.

Then, just as we were packed and ready to get back in the car, I heard a whisper.

"Thank you, Daddy, for trying to show us a good time. We love you."

Quick and to the heart.

As we marched to the car, I was still mad. But my anger was turning entirely inward. In the car I heard sniffles from the back seat. Then a tiny voice said, "Daddy, are you mad at us?"

"No," I replied through the swelling in my throat. "I'm mad at myself."

"Why, Daddy?"

"I just wish I were a better father."

The guilt is strong in my family, uncontrollable, used like a switch but cutting so much deeper. Crocodile tears flowed, and I felt like the lowest form of scum on earth.

The whole event lasted no more than ten minutes from the time we started building the kites to the point that we drove off in tears. I fear, as would any parent, that the event may last a lifetime in their memories. Something for which I will be paying their therapist and mine for years to come.

But at home we sat on the couch and talked. They nuzzled up close, unafraid of the big scary monster, a child on each side in the crooks of my arms. They fit perfectly in there, like we were all designed to fit together, so comfortable. Tears streamed down my face now, and I summoned an apology from somewhere deep inside my soul. They looked at me with enormous, forgiving blue eyes and told me it was ok. They smiled and, like the Grinch, my heart grew three sizes that day. It was perhaps the most grownup conversation I've ever had.

Of course by this time the clouds had cleared and the day was as crisp and beautiful as it had been just an hour earlier. Never fails.

We spent the rest of the day outside; the kids playing, doing a dance recital just for their dad. And me, watching them with such wonder and awe, licking my wounds, amazed at a child's enormous capacity for forgiveness.

Humble ourselves like little children. Another one of those Bible figures told us to do that. And now I know why.

April 4, 2009

❦

The Substance of Things Hoped For

I CAN be a creature of habit.

I set my slippers in the same place every night to easily put them on first thing in the morning. I buy my steaks only at the Handy Market. I drink Mai Tais only when I'm at Damon's.

And each Sunday morning at church I sit in the same pew in the same spot – so long as no one has gotten there before me, which I take every effort to prevent. I've gotten used to this seat. It's a place where I'm comfortable and not distracted by any new things or people around me. In fact, I find that most people sit in the same place in church.

The pews face north. And every Sunday morning the sun rises and shines through the tall, narrow stained glass windows on the eastern wall of the sanctuary. And a shaft of light beams down upon my seat. It hits others around me too, but I like to think that I am its target.

Last week, Easter Sunday, that light made its faithful appearance, bathing me as I pondered what we were there celebrating. Namely, that this person Jesus, who was both God and man, rose from the dead 2000 years ago so everyone would be forgiven their transgressions and believe that there is a supreme being willing to die for them.

Many good people don't share my belief however. Some claim it in differing ways and others claim no belief at all. But even the latter have faith, I would argue. And that's different. They have faith not in spiritual realms but in personal, corporeal or empirical ones.

The faith I have is real; as real as the weather, oxygen, and the fact that the Dodgers will slump at the end of this season leaving me disappointed until next spring. That this faith is real to me does not eliminate my doubt and questioning though. On the contrary. Someone once said that doubt is not the opposite of faith but a requirement of it. And I find great solace in that. To paraphrase Frederick Beuchner, faith is best understood as a verb, not a noun; as something we exercise rather than a concept we possess. That's why we go through trials. Faith must be fed daily, and it's favorite food is our human struggle.

I wasn't raised in the church. I didn't have a foxhole moment, a great parting of the clouds or 12-step program that led me here. No, I arrived after wandering through life sampling a smidgen of this and that along the way. I've lit incense at Buddhist temples and removed my shoes at ashrams. At times I thought Plato or Rumi or Shirley MacLaine had it all figured out. In the mid-90s I spent more than a few nights harmonically converging with a bottle of cheap merlot, listening to Yanni and reading New Age stories of people "embracing the light" by the "seat of their soul."

Just as something causes our hearts and lungs to begin moving and continue for the rest of our lifetime, something causes us all to seek; to seek things daily that make us feel safe, secure and comforted in an unpredictable world. And this seeking requires faith in something we can't touch. Maybe it's faith in science and mathematics. Faith in your own ingenuity. Faith in appointed government officials. Faith in another person that you think knows more than you do. Faith in the Glendale Beeline or Burbank Bus schedules. Faith in a bottle of tequila or syringe of heroin. But all are ways of seeking peace of mind or body.

I reached out to some readers to get their thoughts, asking them what they had faith in.

Sylvie Madore has faith in simply doing good. "If I'm good to my body," she said, "it'll be good to me. If I do good work, work will be good to me. If I'm good to my neighbors, they'll be good to me. Maybe not right away. Often in an unexpected way. But it will happen…Not because the bible says so, not because that's the way to get into heaven someday. [But] because it's good for me right here, right now. Everyday."

Mark Lytle has "no faith in my car or in any mechanics of any sort in the whole universe." But thinks that, "hope plus perseverance plus good luck plus will can be a worldly kind of faith… I have faith that my plane will get off the ground…But, it's not just probability, it's knowing and feeling that these things will happen, even though logically they could stop at any time. Because they have to [go on] for us to go on."

Faith doesn't "prove" anything. But it does point. It points to something that makes us say, "That! 'That Thing' makes me suspend my doubt and disbelief. Maybe it's the way the numbers fall together so perfectly, the orderliness of my routine, the way she composes herself or the way he carries that cross. But whatever it is, it makes me feel better about tomorrow. And maybe the next day."

I want to devote a little time to this; to bring you the occasional story of those who seek and have faith in whatever form comforts them. Maybe you'll agree with what you read, maybe you won't. But I hope in some way you understand yourself or others a little bit better through these stories.

Everyone's looking for that seat in the light, hoping it hits them so they can feel the warmth and security it brings. What do you have faith in?

April 10, 2010

❦

Faith in the Ability to Get By

Broken bottle glass sparkles by the roadside,
But not nearly as brightly as my spirits.

Fence rails march in orderly fashion
Toward Oklahoma City, but
My heart does a wild fandango on its way.
Telephone wires race to beat me there, not knowing
My thought baggage arrived almost two months ago
And the rest of me now hurries after.

IT WAS 10:00 pm when Lori Spring got the call. On the other end of the line was a musician, one of the "loves of her life." Come to Oklahoma City, he beckoned, and drive back to the west coast with me. So she took her tip jar to the nearest open liquor store, cashed it in and boarded a train that night.

It was only enough to get her to Mesa, Arizona, with nothing left for food, emergencies or a return trip. But there she was able to cash in a savings bond that hadn't yet matured, thanks to a gentleman bank teller wanting to help a pretty young lady. She boarded the next bus and along the way scribbled poetry in her notebook, capturing the landscape she saw passing outside. As well as the landscape within. At the end of the road she found her musician. And in some ways herself.

When I ask Lori, now Lori McCaffery, what enabled her to make such a journey without hesitation or fear of the unknown, she doesn't think long. "I guess I would say I have faith in my ability to keep going." And it's a credo she still lives by to this day, almost 50 years after that wild fandango across the Southwest.

"I have faith in my ability to cope," she told me over cherry pie at the Marie Callendar's. "My mother always told me, 'figure it out, use your ingenuity.' If I heard that once, I heard it a thousand times growing up."

Lori's single mother worked in a dime store to provide for her three children. Her father came and went, but eventually went for good. Raised in Longview, Washington, Lori recalls picking strawberries to earn money for school clothes.

A high school art teacher would be one of the great influences in Lori's life, a teacher who didn't exactly conform to the norms of the day. "She was totally different in this small town," Lori recalls. "She smoked in the classroom, blowing it out the window. She cussed. 'Damn the torpedoes was always her attitude." And she saw something special in Lori, eventually helping her to get a scholarship to college and a ticket out of her small town life.

Though tuition was taken care of, Lori arrived at college without a place to live. "I didn't know that you were supposed to do that in advance...In a lot of ways I was very naïve, and still am." No problem. Within a couple hours of getting off the train, Lori found a room in a private residence and was on her way into the world of higher education.

It's this combination of serendipity, ingenuity, force of will and simply being a pleasant person, that has seen Lori through all that life throws in one's way.

"And working harder than anyone else," she adds.

She's been a waitress, a folk club manager, Sears mail order accounting clerk, a private detective's Girl Friday and more. For the last 40 years she's been an event coordinator for the same large cathedral in Hancock Park. Such longevity at a job is rare these days.

But time doesn't always bring harmony. After her 20 year first marriage ended, she met a man she thought might be the one to spend the rest of her life with. The only problem was he lived in London. After some serious soul-searching, strategic planning with her ex and financial finagling – unlike her youthful fandango – she moved to London to see if her gut was right. She was back without missing her daughter's next birthday, and brought Colin home with her. They've been married now for 21 years.

To say Lori's view on life is rosy wouldn't be accurate. She knows that for every rose there's a thorn, and life is a constant series of highs and lows, struggles and successes. You just need to keep moving forward. She lives with lupus, the potential to soon be phased out of her job and, like the rest of us, the task of getting by day to day financially and emotionally. But somehow, you can't imagine any of this ever getting her down.

"I intend to go skydiving for my 75th birthday. If George Bush can do it, by God, I can do it."

Once Lori got to Oklahoma City she found out that her paramour had two other ladies he wanted to bring back with them. The thrill of young love and that spontaneous life adventure would fade on the drive back; four people and their luggage heading west in a crowded Volkswagen Bug. That musician would soon move on and so would Lori.

There are grey areas in life, times when you simply need to dive in even though you don't know what's going to happen; situations and occurrences that fall beyond meaning and words. But if you don't roll the dice, you can't play in the game. And you have to believe that by simply playing, you're winning.

"I have faith in having faith, I guess."

A faith born of necessity, hardened by strife, and perfected by an immutable hope that she'll be around for more tomorrow. With that, nothing is insurmountable.

She looked and looked at the storm-black sky
And couldn't visualize it blue.
But still somewhere down deep within her
She knew the sun would shine again.

April 24, 2010

❧

Faith in Science, Creativity and Invention

"Although nature commences with reason and ends in experience it is necessary for us to do the opposite, that is to commence with experience and from this to proceed to investigate the reason." — Leonardo da Vinci

FAITH comes in many forms, I believe. And in my search to find it in places unexpected, I'm learning a lot.

I sat down with Steve Hines at Shaker's for breakfast one recent morning to further my exploration. Steve's an inventor, and I asked him what he had faith in. He handed me a photocopied page from Webster's Dictionary. Of the various definitions listed for the word faith, Steve had underlined the following: "Belief in something for which there is no proof."

"[Faith is] not a word that I use very much at all," he told me. "It's hardly in my vocabulary because it's not a part of my objective activity in quantifying things. I just don't think that way."

Faith and science are strange bedfellows to be sure. And that definition of faith is something I would agree with.

"I come from a science and engineering background and deal with facts and measurable, quantifiable data," Steve told me.

But if we're open to another definition — that faith is a will we exercise rather than a concept we possess; something that points to a thing in which we put our trust and hope — I wondered what I might find.

Born and raised in North Carolina, Steve came west 30 years ago by way of New York and London, bringing with him a vast knowledge of engineering and physics. After stints with Kodak and Disney, he created his own company, HinesLab (www.HinesLab.com), where he creates prototypes for image displays and develops optical and mechanical devices for photographic equipment and flight simulators. He's currently working on a way to view 3-D TV without wearing glasses, the Holy Grail of 3-D technology today.

"Optical engineering is so appealing because light is beautiful to work with. You can break it up into so many colors and prisms . . . I love working with it."

In short, he's a man who helps us see the world in new and vibrant ways.

When we talk about who inspires him, Steve's response is quick and obvious: da Vinci. He admires the Renaissance man's free thinking, his strength and vision in the worlds of science and of art. It's hard for me to reconcile that one person can be so accomplished in what to my mind would be divergent disciplines, art and science.

But Steve sees no conflict in the two.

"Engineering can be very creative. There's plenty of creative engineering in a digital camera, a suspension bridge or the space station."

Like da Vinci, Steve is a lover of music and art, and finds beauty everywhere in the physical world. He draws and is a photographer in his own right.

Is there a way to measure beauty, whether in art or the eye of the beholder?

"Objectivity takes a holiday when you are trying to critique a painting or something."

At the heart of any inventor, whether artist or scientist, is the desire to discover; to pull from some combination of the known and experiential, and the ether of what is not yet known, something never before seen. There is a craving for that moment when a new way to look at the world has been brought forth in words, sound or light.

"At the moment of invention, the thrill is exhilarating, almost ecstatic."

Perhaps that's what I'm looking for. Call it the "moment of invention," or the "creative spark," or the "a-ha" moment. It may hit you when you're in the shower, when you're writing or reading or jogging; when your mind is free and wanders in imagination. Or when you're in your laboratory focused on the way a beam of light hits a lens.

It's the birth of the idea, or that idea's fulfillment. Words fit together to elicit an emotion in a new way; colors on a canvas stir something in our souls; beams of light do what you wanted and prove your hypothesis.

Maybe that's where I see faith in anyone whose life is devoted to invention and creativity in any form — a combination of trust and hope that the immeasurable moment of discovery will come again. And that's what keeps them going.

Does he think there's anything beyond the physical, measurable world?

"No."

But he adds, "There is one thing that I wish I had an answer for: infinity. Physical infinity, in space. I would love to know what that's all about. How could it possibly go forever? Surely there's got to be a wall there somewhere. I can't deal with it. It fries my circuits. So I quit thinking about it. There's an unknown right there."

He points his hope and his knowledge in the direction of creation, invention and discovery. In a world of facts and raw data he sees beauty that can't be quantified and a place that can't be touched. Is faith somewhere in there? I'm not sure. But passion certainly is.

And we could all learn a thing or two from such passion.

May 22, 2010

∿

Faith in the American Dream

WHEN Art Chudabala was a boy, his father took him on weekly fishing ventures off the Southern California coast. On one of these excursions his father caught a huge mackerel and hauled it on deck.

His father immediately filleted it and took a bite of the raw, still-warm flesh.

"There was blood running down his cheeks," he told me. "That was hardcore."

Art, a Burbank resident, recalled this story as we left the fishmonger's stall at the farmer's market and perused the other vendors looking for his next meal's muse.

"My pops is my inspiration," Art told me.

Though his father died five years ago, Art channels him whenever he's in the kitchen.

"He was the best cook in the family. My mom, God bless her, is good. But my dad, he took it somewhere else. He was a very Zen, patient guy in life. Same with cooking. He wouldn't do a thing without prepping. I got that from him. It's the whole process."

Art's parents immigrated to the U.S. from Thailand in the late 1960s seeking the opportunities this country had to offer. They established a little takeout restaurant in North Hollywood that Art would work at in the summer. They'd also cater outdoor festivals and open-air markets.

"I was out there at 11 years old selling won-tons and egg rolls and stuff like that."

It's a business his family still runs. Art seriously considered culinary school before he went into show business.

His film and TV credits as an actor and editor are impressive. But, of Art's talents, cooking is perhaps his most natural and effortless.

"Cooking is something I've always done well but never really focused on. I was the guy that everyone wanted to be roommates with because we could have a piece of bologna, a can of mushroom soup and beer, and I'd cook up something good."

Though he's a skilled artisan when taking on someone else's character or cutting scenes to enhance someone else's artistic expression, in the kitchen, something else is allowed to take over— something true, sincere and gracious: Art. The craft and the man, pure and simple.

And it has him reevaluating life, looking at the things we've all taken for granted.

"For me food was always a passion. When I get home and get to cook, it's a way for me to go Zen, a way for me to exhale."

Art's recent soul-searching may be because he finds himself at the crossroads of 40. Or it may have something to do with a recent and unexpected opportunity to showcase his skills as a chef for one of the most famous grill masters in the world.

Coaxed by a friend, Art submitted an audition video to the Food Network. His passion and comfort in front of the camera and behind the grill came through. From thousands of entries by amateur chefs around the country, Art became one of the few selected to prepare his own recipe side-by-side with Bobby Flay on his show "Grill It with Bobby Flay."

What did Art prepare for the Iron Chef, restaurateur and Food Network star? Thai BBQ chicken, a recipe handed down to him by his father.

The episode is now airing on the Food Network. To see Art's audition video, look him up on Facebook.

"Yeah, it was great to get on the show. But for me it was way bigger than the show. When I act, I'm playing a character. That food thing was totally different. I've never been myself on camera. And on top of that, I brought my family, my culture, my history, the way I grew up Asian American, and why I cook Asian fusion. That was me."

Watching the episode, it's hard not to like the affable and witty amateur chef as he cuts it up with Flay.

"My recipes are very much a diary," he said. "Like you listen to a piece of music and it takes you back to a particular time. That's what food does for me."

And it's hard not to get hungry watching him.

Ask anyone why they like to cook, and you'll get a lot of answers. Perhaps the most common thread is a desire to share; to have a vision, see it to completion, offer it to others and see them wordlessly experience what you envisioned. With cooking, your work is consumed physically, rather than cerebrally, literally becoming a part of the recipient in the most unselfish way.

"Yeah, and I did that," Art told me. "For an Iron Chef. And I rocked him."

When I asked Art what he has faith in, he hesitated.

"This is going to sound corny," he told me. "But I still have faith in the American dream. I come from an immigrant family. This country has given me everything, every opportunity, the highs and the lows. I still believe in that very much. And even more so now than ever."

Like most everyone today, work has been a struggle for Art lately.

"I don't really know what's going to happen tomorrow, like me and the rest of this country, and the world. But I still have faith. I mean seriously... I went on the Food Network! Where else are you ever going to be able to do that? I'm just some cat. At 40 I can say to myself, 'I'm going to switch gears and do something completely different.' Where else can I even think of doing something else altogether? Yeah, I still have faith in the American dream. I do. As Americans you can never lose that sense of hope."

Art paused.

"And all because I barbecued some chicken."

July 31, 2010

Run for the Roses of the World

"When you do nothing, you feel overwhelmed and powerless. But when you get involved, you feel the sense of hope and accomplishment that comes from knowing you are working to make things better." — Maya Angelou

ACCORDING to the American Cancer Society, almost one in 8 women in the United States will be diagnosed with breast cancer in their lifetime

Rose Marie Hunt had beaten breast cancer once. But when it came back, and metastasized to other parts of her body, Jessica Cribbs knew her mother's prognosis wasn't good. A Burbank resident for eight years, Jessica had already gone back to her hometown of Petersburg, Mich. — a farming community of 1,120 people somewhere between Toledo and Ann Arbor — to be with her mother through radiation and chemotherapy.

But when "quality of life" became the topic of discussion rather than longevity, Jessica, her husband and two children made the long drive back East for what she knew would be the last Christmas with the matriarch and center of her family.

Jessica set up a blog (*www.strengthofarose.com*) for her mother to update family and friends on her progress. But Rose was soon too sick to keep it up. Jessica took over, and the blog became a daughter's way to share what it's like losing a mother to cancer.

On a cold, Midwestern winter's day in January 2009, Rose, at the far-too-young age of 54, took her last breath surrounded by her family, holding her daughter's hand.

"I know people like to think death might be peaceful," Jessica told me last week as she rocked her sleeping newborn on the dining room table. "But it wasn't. It was not peaceful watching. "

Jessica was afraid these last, painful moments would be all she had left of her mother, her best friend, the person who taught her everything she knew about being a mom, a friend and a daughter. Her mother's death did rock Jessica's world for some time.

"But it's amazing when you get through that, what you're left with," Jessica said. "All the things from childhood, things she said. I'll be in the kitchen cooking something and remember who taught me the recipe. Or the clothes that I'm wearing that she got me the last birthday I had with her."

Rose spent most of her energy thinking about and helping others, Jessica said. "Everything I am is what she's left me with. She was my model. A pretty amazing model."

So Jessica was determined that her mother's unselfish legacy be remembered. She vowed to make things better. Just like her mother always did.

"I'm not one to sit and mope," she told me. "So I knew I wanted to do good things in her name."

That's how Jessica came up with the idea to hold a 5K run/walk in her mother's honor — the Rose Run (*www.theroserun.com*).

Jessica wanted to do what she could to help find a cure for breast cancer in her lifetime, and certainly within the lifetime of her two daughters. Held on Community Day in Petersburg, the Rose Run raised more than $10,000 in 2009. Jessica got almost twice the 175 participants she had anticipated.

This year she's hoping to exceed her expectations once again. While Jessica will be in Michigan for the Rose Run in her hometown, there will be a simultaneous virtual 5K Rose Run here in Griffith Park next Saturday morning, July 17, thanks in part to Moms in Motion (*www.momsinmotion.com*), a global social network connecting moms through fitness.

All of the proceeds go directly to the nonprofit Breast Cancer Research Foundation. (The American Cancer Society estimated that in 2009, about 192,370 new cases of invasive breast cancer would be diagnosed among women in the U.S., and that 40,170 would die from the disease. There are about 2.5 million breast cancer survivors in the U.S. today. I'd wager most of us know at least one of these brave women.

"It's like when you get a new car," Jessica said. "You suddenly notice that everyone else now has the same car. Now that I've been affected by cancer, I see everybody has been affected by cancer. And

I really want to encourage people to do something healthy and take accountability right now."

She's living up to the qualities her mother instilled in her.

Rose Marie Hunt was a country girl, raised on the farm, the same one Jessica was raised on. Born in the same house that she died in. And always putting others before herself.

"She was just thoughtful," Jessica said of her mother. "It was never about her. She was forgiving more than anybody I knew. She was strong. She had tiny hands that could do anything. She was just amazing. You really don't know how amazing until she's gone."

When Jessica knew there was no beating the cancer, she had the hardest conversation of her life. She asked her mother what she wanted for her family after she was gone. And Rose told her.

"Be happy. Be a family. That's it."

Rose had her priorities straight.

July 10, 2010

A Sheep in Sheep's Clothing

AS A columnist, I'm given some latitude in expressing how I feel while reporting the facts. I do so in hopes that my thoughts will resonate with readers and, agree or not, generate productive dialogue.

With this in mind, let me tell you how I feel about a vampire book author's renunciation of Christianity and fur coats.

An uproar on Facebook trickled into mainstream media recently. Anne Rice, a Christian and the only living author of vampire books worth reading, formally announced that she has "... quit Christianity in the name of Christ."

To summarize, she said: "I remain committed to Christ as always, but not to being 'Christian' or to being part of Christianity.

It's simply impossible for me to 'belong' to this quarrelsome, hostile, disputatious, and deservedly infamous group ..."

She refuses to be "anti-gay," "anti-feminist," "anti-artificial birth control," "anti-Democrat," "anti-secular humanism," "anti-science" and "anti-life."

She continued: "Following Christ does not mean following His followers. Christ is infinitely more important than Christianity and always will be, no matter what Christianity is, has been, or might become."

While somewhat over-generalizing and not reflective of many denominations' views, her description of "Christianity" is a commonly held stereotype. And in my humble opinion, more accurate than not.

The response Rice is getting emphasizes the schism within this quarrelsome and hostile group. As a public figure, her words add fuel to this bonfire. She could have kept her spiritual struggles private. But she didn't. And I'm glad. Because I agree with her. Mostly.

I too want to divorce the flawed and fractious manmade institution, disassociate myself from its politicized views and hypocrisy. But I cannot renounce its people. I could no more deny certain embarrassing relatives than I could certain opinionated members of the collective church. But I will disagree with them.

The church is people. Not a building, an organization, a dogma or the formal written declarations of a few. To embrace Christ — within a formal institution or in one's heart — is a personal and therefore unique relationship. But not private.

To accept that relationship is to accept the collection of imperfect, damaged and misinformed followers he's gathered. The disciples, a motley and disputatious group themselves, didn't get to choose who made the final 12. Neither do we. Jesus went out of his way to gather a bunch of self-centered and disagreeable people; to befriend and defend the disenfranchised. So must we.

I'm one sheep in a big flock. And many in that flock are fighting to prevent a segment of our society from using the word "married" to define their union. With the overturning of Proposition 8 this week, the battle is sure to continue for some time.

As an American, as a Christian, I have no right to tell someone else whom they may or may not marry. Especially a group so systematically ostracized from the church as to feel unwanted by their very maker. Whether homosexuality is a sin isn't the debate. Civil rights is the debate.

To argue that same-sex marriage will deteriorate the institution of marriage is a frail argument at best. A quick survey of my divorced family members and friends shows that we heterosexuals have done a pretty good job of that ourselves. Adultery, which remains legal in California, is a far greater threat to the sanctity of marriage than whether my friends Rick and Rick get to walk down the aisle and legally seal their lifelong commitment to each other.

It's rightfully argued that Proposition 8 passed "by the will of the people" (52.3% of voters to be exact). Well, even majorities get it wrong sometimes. It took a four-year Civil War to convince the majority of people in the Confederacy that slavery was wrong, and quite a few more years to give African Americans equal rights under the Constitution. Women weren't granted the same rights as men until just 90 years ago.

And in both cases, the Bible was used to defend their subjugation. Today we know that this was an incorrect interpretation of scripture at that time in history. But are we now saying we've caught every vague biblical interpretation and, unfortunately, the rights of non-heterosexuals didn't get in under the deadline?

The separation of church and state is a mutually beneficial arrangement sacred to our God-given and constitutional rights. If you don't believe in God, no one can force their views upon you.

Jesus didn't.

And while I'm at it, let me get this off my chest — 8,000 or 8 zillion years, I don't care when or how the Earth was created. If God himself devoted only one of 1,189 chapters in his book to this topic, why are his followers so obsessed with it?

Many Christians religiously tune in to Fox News as if it were God's Own Network. They quote Glenn, Rush, Bill and Sean more than Matthew, Mark, Luke and John. Frankly, I feel Fox News is merely ratings-seeking, ad-revenue-generating sensationalism disguised as news to exploit a rabid fan base.

In the spirit of equal time, I think MSNBC is the lower-rated left-wing equivalent, just as toxic and one-sided. Which is why so many people now get their news from Comedy Central.

Jesus seemed to hate labels — neither Jew nor Greek. Try imagining him telling an honest seeker, "This may not be the right church for you," because you're liberal, gay or social justice; because you listen to NPR, voted for Obama or against Proposition 8.

I'm a Christian. Not a conservative, not a liberal. Neither right nor left, Republican nor Democrat. Just a Christian — the noun, not the adjective.

There. I'm out of the closet. I'm taking off my wolf-skin-fur-coat stereotype of what it means to be Christian. I'm a sheep in a very diverse flock — a sheep in sheep's clothing.

Disagree with me.

August 7, 2010

౮❦

Prayers Not Answered on a Schedule

Part 1 of Maggie's Story

WHEN Marguerite Beck was 5, she prayed for God to make it snow. Though infrequent, snow in the foothills of La Crescenta wasn't unheard of. She awoke the next day to a blanket of white covering her neighborhood. Raised by a devoutly Catholic mother, Marguerite prayed often after that.

"Mass every Sunday," she told me. "No meat on Fridays, confession at least every two weeks and usually daily mass during Lent. All major church holidays were attended in full regalia."

Even beyond the rituals, Marguerite felt a special connection to her god.

Her parents' marriage lasted 50 years, something she attributes to her mother's religious faith. Though it wasn't "Ozzie and Harriet," Marguerite looks back fondly, especially toward a mother she calls her "she-ro." Self-admittedly naïve and a prude, Marguerite always strived to do what was right in her faith and family.

"I was constantly afraid of what people would think of me and mostly I just never wanted to hurt anyone. My job in this world was to be the peacemaker within my family and without."

At 20, Marguerite fell in love, married and set out to become the best mother she could be, just like the woman who raised her. She describes her life in the lyrics of a Mary Chapin Carpenter song:

"She does the carpool, she PTAs. Doctors and dentists, she drives all day. When she was 29 she delivered number three. And every Christmas card showed a perfect family. Everything runs right on time, years of practice and design. Spit and polish till it shines."

Yet, there was a stirring under that shine, yearnings Marguerite felt almost all her life, but couldn't explain or express. When she met and grew close to a like-minded choir director at church, those stirrings finally emerged.

That choir director was the rector's wife.

Though she admits to having crushes on both boys and girls when she was young, she attributed the more confusing feelings for girls to being a tomboy. Her Catholic upbringing and conservative Christian family life told her such desires were unnatural and evil. As her feelings for the rector's wife grew, these admonitions haunted her.

"I was swimming in thoughts and emotions of doubt and fear...I was beaten down by my own fears and my own homophobia."

Her husband was obviously shocked when Marguerite told him about her long-dormant emotions. When Christian psychotherapy didn't "cure" her, Marguerite stopped going to church altogether, too ashamed and fearful anyone would find out.

But what persecution she feared from her brethren was nothing compared to that which she heaped upon herself.

"I thought I would burn in hell...or burst into flames if I stepped inside [a church]," she said.

She felt ostracized and abandoned by the only thing that gave her peace and sanity — her Christianity. Over the next year, she went back and forth, reconciling with her husband, but never able to reconcile with herself. She knew something had to change.

"I witnessed the difficulty of my parents' relationship and of them being stuck. I didn't want that for me and I didn't want my kids to have to deal with seeing that... I just wasn't prepared for the drama or the pain or the hiding or the lies that would ensue."

Faced with the choice of doing what one thinks is best for themselves or best for their children, most parents opt for the latter. So with no other choice as she saw it, that's what Marguerite did.

"I ended up leaving without my children so that [my ex] wouldn't tell them about my homosexuality. I just didn't want them to hate me." And she was certain they would.

Too young to understand such things, her three sons rationalized that Mom left because Dad was mean; an easy conclusion for her oldest son. One night, though he should have been in bed, he overheard his mother crying.

"I'm certain he assumed that if I was crying, his father must be saying something hurtful."

But that wasn't the case.

"I was probably crying from guilt, from indecision, from just not knowing what to do," she said.

There's nothing inspirational or life-affirming to write about the destruction of a family. Nothing to glamorize about divorce. Under any circumstances, it's a tragedy.

With the guidance and instruction of a faithful life, Marguerite did what she thought best; only she knows the feelings inside her heart and soul that would bring her to leave a seemingly perfect marriage to seek peace with herself.

That was 25 years ago. On life's journey, we cry out for easy directions, clearly marked signposts to guide us. Like rest stops, we don't always get them when we want them. Every answered prayer, every destination, directs us down some new road.

Yet prayers are always answered. Sometimes it's "yes." Sometimes "no." And sometimes "wait."

October 9, 2010

The Search for Commonality

Part 2 of Maggie's Story

MARGUERITE doesn't pray for snow anymore.

"Let's just say for the past 25 years, the only time I pray is when I'm taking off or hit turbulence in an airplane."

It took years for Marguerite to reconcile the conflict between her feelings and her faith. In the end, faith lost.

"I'm not sure what that higher power looks like, or if it only consists of finding the higher power within my own being. I may fall somewhere into the agnostic category these days."

She and the rector's wife created a life together, learning to navigate the world anew in light of their sexuality. Visits with her sons were bittersweet.

"We tried to make it as normal as possible ... But it was always hard when they had to go. It wasn't fair to their dad because it was most always fun when they came to visit us, and then he got them back for school, homework, punishments, etc."

"Normal" also meant continuing to hide her sexuality from her family. They eventually found a community of people with similar stories — many more tragic than theirs — helping them to find comfort and acceptance in themselves. When she finally decided to break her silence, she told her oldest son first, when he graduated high school.

"Interestingly, when I revealed my sexuality to [him], he said he was glad he didn't know the real reason at the time, because it would have been beyond his capability to deal with it at his age. So I guess I'm glad I waited."

Marguerite then told everyone in her family. She says the reactions were unanimous.

"Well, duh. As long as you're happy, we're happy. We love you."

As happens when any marriage dissolves, hurtful words were spoken that can never be taken back. But Marguerite credits her ex for raising their sons to be the wonderful individuals they are today.

"It was difficult on us both. I understand this was a very emotional and hurtful time for him as well, and he was just trying to preserve and protect his own being and do what he thought best for our children. He's an extraordinary individual, which is what led me to marry him in the first place."

It was never easy, but they can all look back with regret, forgiveness and love.

"It has taken a while, but we are an extended family. It speaks to the people we've all become."

Of the rector's wife — still her soul mate and life partner — Marguerite speaks with honeymoon tones.

"I've never felt the type of spiritual bond or love of another human being as I feel with [her]. She can love me more in one minute than any man could love me in a lifetime."

Like any relationship, they've had their ups and downs.

"The old tapes in my head have told me for so many years that I wasn't good enough or didn't deserve her love. But I do. We all deserve this kind of love."

Would they marry if it were legal? Of course. But they don't need a document or a word to validate their feelings, she said.

"Truthfully, I don't care if it's called marriage — keep marriage for church — or civil unions ... I just would like the same rights I would have if I married a man."

As she sees it, there's hypocrisy in a religious culture that fights against same-sex marriage while other factors are truly responsible for the institution's erosion.

"Britney Spears can be married for 18 hours, Liz Taylor can marry as many men as she wants, and people will only shake their heads and forget about it." Then she adds sarcastically, "But couple a man and man or a woman to another woman? What's the world coming too?"

Hypocrisy. Selfishness. Fear. Control. Resent. Sounds like a recipe for our human condition. At the heart of our laws and norms, beliefs and spiritual dogma are the people who created them — none better, smarter or more spiritually evolved than another. All equally flawed.

When I started this, I was looking for an answer. I don't think I got it. As a Christian myself, I was saddened that Marguerite lost her faith, and that's what drove me to explore this. I want her to have all the joy and rights as everyone else.

But I also understand why others, led by conservative Christians, oppose this. They quote the adage "love the sinner, hate the sin," to clarify their beliefs. Sadly, that only serves the one who hates. It's not a very inviting slogan to the one it's aimed at.

My prayer is that by focusing on a person, we can find some commonality in this debate. If we can, maybe those who believe in God will get that much closer to him. And those who don't will respect believers as they do everyone else.

This may work for some, but I know it won't for most. Mankind clings to its hatred like a security blanket. And that saddens me the most.

October 16, 2010

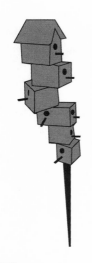

Rivers

Nothing in the world is as soft and yielding as water,
yet nothing can better overcome the hard and strong,
for they can neither control nor do away with it.

~ from the Tao Te Ching

Life is a process of becoming,
a combination of states we have to go through.
Where people fail is that they wish to elect a state
and remain in it.
This is a kind of death.

~ Anaïs Nin

Drifting

THERE is a river near my house. It starts as a clandestine spring we'll never find atop some far off mountain to the north, joins with other trickles and wells as it travels downhill. It ends somewhere to the south, past the glass and metal and cement, in an ocean we can't see from here.

And on its journey it cuts straight through the hearts of cities and people and time. It passes by my home, and yours. It runs through neighborhoods, past schools and ranches, power plants, soccer fields and playgrounds; alongside streets, freeways and rail yards; past buildings that will be long gone as she still wanders through the lives of our children. And their children.

This particular river has walls of concrete, sheer, high and impenetrable in places, sloping and easy to climb in others. Its bed too is concrete, save in places where land has risen through the cracks. Life has a way of doing that in the city. But it is a river, make no mistake.

It roams through our lives taking away our waste, the dust washed clean by occasional, welcoming rain. And anything else we cast aside or want to be rid of.

Runoff it's called, the water that flows through this river. An appropriate word, runoff, for the things we no longer want or have use of; the things we can't bear to look at again. The rain and the river's flow will take it all away and downriver, run it off. It's polluted and murky, this river. But it can't be killed. Nor can the life it sustains. And we force ourselves to remember no more that what we cast away into that river — what we chase off because we no longer want — eventually comes back in the form of rain atop some mountain to the north.

It is a river, as much as any other, bringing nourishment, healing and peace; but also wrath, destruction and decay. It can be redirected, channeled, dammed even. But it cannot be stopped.

Throughout, the pavement gives way to a real riverbed, where the constant, peaceful attack of rushing water has taken its toll;

where life in the form of land, trees and grass has taken root, planted itself firmly against the currents. Chains of lush islands have formed amongst the urban sprawl; sanctuaries, oases that give rest and protection for travelers as they drift downstream.

Giant stalks of bamboo reach into the sky, thick clusters more dense than cornfields, two, maybe three stories high. Oak trees and elm. Great blossoms of tall grass seize these islands, the kind one might see a machete taken to in the jungle. Vast clusters of marsh-weed and succulent moss carpet the water's bed. And palm trees, palm trees everywhere, great and small.

The tallest of trees, those that peer high enough to see beyond the cement channel walls, bend south with the wind, pointing down the river. The grass and low-lying plant life too, aim south with the ceaseless flow of water. Directing us to the inevitable end. And beyond.

Great blue heron and snowy egret stand motionless on crooked legs waiting to strike at some glimmering below the surface. Ducks and geese swim against the current, seemingly motionless. Coot and teal wade through the shallows.

And I think I even saw a hawk once, soaring in spirals overhead, watching, always watching.

Look closely, get down and walk her banks and there's more. Bass, carp and sunfish; tilapia and of course waste-eating, bottom-dwelling catfish. I hear steelhead trout were once plentiful here, though that time is long gone. And yet people still fish here, for pleasure or survival.

There's a place along the river we're told not to pass. Though I can see the uncluttered path beyond, the signs on the fence say the path is closed. Yet, nothing prevents us from going around that fence. The signs tell us not to proceed, but they look away, begging us to disobey.

I do. And I see what's been hidden.

The islands and the trees are even greater here. I didn't know they could be. Freeways and warehouses are replaced by neighborhoods again. Small rapids here, serene pools there. Silent in places where the trees are thick and the river hidden. So loud elsewhere it drowns out the other river, of cars, helicopters, sirens, and low rumbling of trains.

Graffiti scars the cement riverbanks, any blank wall begging to be a canvas for the screams of misguided youth. But also a reminder that others have been here before me, and will be here when I'm gone.

Homeless men and women call the river home. The path is their street, the islands and shade trees their front yard. Their pilfered shopping carts and rickety bikes are built out to carry everything they possess and gather throughout their long days. They sleep in dry storm drains during summer months, under shanty tarps and cardboard when the weather is less kind. They seem to wander the banks by day without purpose. But they have one: holding back the enemy time for just one more day.

Teenagers sit on the concrete banks high above the water's edge, watching the world go by. They've nothing better to do. When you pass, they watch you through sideways glances, quickly hiding what's in their hands. A love note? Cigarette? Magazine? Needle? They seek refuge here, sharing a first kiss, a joint or perhaps more in the safety of the islands' dense cover. Refuge from an angry world, abusive father, crying mother. We all had places like this when we were their age, even if only a state of mind.

Families roam the riverbanks in slow, ambling stride. They picnic under the shade of towering eucalyptus; gather to laugh where there is grass to sit.

Little ones in strollers who don't know of the river yet; an old man with his walker makes the long, painful trek from his home just a block away. He sits under the shade of a birch tree watching the waters run. Unlike me, he can see the river's end.

Look just right, through squinted eyes, and this could be a tributary to the Amazon or Nile. Widen your gaze and you know exactly where you are. The city of angels.

Why are we drawn to the river, I wonder. To sit in contemplation and look upon waters, still or running? To streams and falls and lakes and oceans? I don't know. But few things give me more peace.

Around the next bend is a boy, not more than five years old, with his father. They sit on the bank of a calm stretch with fishing poles pointed in the air, like antennae seeking signals of life. The boy doesn't know why, but the father does. The boy, with energy to spare, can hardly sit still, yammering and quizzing his father, who answers him tolerantly and gladly. I can't hear what they're talking about, but I'm sure it's as innocent as it is important.

Then a strike.

In shock, the boy grabs his rod as dad cheers. Judging from his father's excitement, this is the boy's first fish. And from the grass and rocks he pulls his silvery catch from the water, finally silent, with no idea what to do next.

I remember that boy.

Giant boulders moved not by machines but by the slow, patient torrent, look to change the river's course. They may succeed, but not for long. The course may change for a moment, redirect to form another stream. But the waters never cease flowing.

I was two years old when he left; the first time a boulder was thrown into the river. Too young to understand what was happening. But that's not the river's concern.

When I became a father and my daughter turned two, I looked at her and tried hard to imagine how it would feel to walk away from her. I had no intention of leaving. But I tried to muster the power to be able to leave her just so I could understand how my father must have felt. And for the briefest mote of time, I felt it. Just for a split second and then it was gone. The thought turned my stomach in a knot as if I'd just jumped out of a plane then suddenly remembered I had no parachute. What effort it would take to repress such a feeling. It made me shudder, wanting to wake myself from a bad dream.

The childhood memories I have of my father are a patchwork of contractually obligated visits — one weekend per month, two weeks in the summer — and a phone call on holidays or birthdays. If he remembered. In these vignettes I was to suck the marrow out of the father-son relationship as quickly as possible before returning home to the protective wings of a mother hen.

When we investigate our past, all we really have are snippets of time, defined memories that stand out in our mind. But there is always an undercurrent, a constant presence like musical montages in a movie — the less remarkable sequences that are just as important for the structure they bring to the story though they may be forgotten. You remember the great scenes, but not necessarily the sequences that show a passage of time between them. Those ordinary moments, those montages sustain and support the truly memorable scenes, provide cohesiveness in the background you may not even be aware of. That's what it's like knowing a parent only on random occasions. No montage, no sense of presence, no reminder that they exist even when you don't see them.

He and his new wife moved on to various towns across the state in those early years. Or at least that's what it seemed like each time I saw him. Each move a step farther away from the four children left behind, his first family. The farther away they went, the more infrequent were our visits.

I loved him and loved visiting him, though he was half-stranger, half-parent. I knew he loved me too, but I felt it in an unfamiliar and un-intimate way. Like loving the empanadas at your favorite Cuban bakery: You crave them when you think about them, consume them greedily when you get them, then don't think about them again until you pass by that bakery and are reminded.

My favorite place to visit him was Catalina Island. You could take a commuter boat across the channel, a big water taxi. Or you could take the seaplane, which was definitely the more exciting and exotic mode of travel. It added an adventurousness to our visits that was missing in everyday relationships. A floating plane, the loud, rumbling propellers harkening back to a ruddier era, the dangerous, turbulent takeoff and flight with the sea and land always still in view. The pilot would let me sit in the cockpit where I could watch the ocean rise to meet us as we descended into Avalon.

My father's house was up a short hill just out of the main village. Everything was in walking distance. One day as we were walking up that hill, sampling various flavors of the fresh saltwater taffy he'd just bought, he stopped without saying anything. He looked over a fence and whistled down into the darkness of a small, eucalyptus shaded valley. He whistled a short call. I had no idea he could whistle like that. How could I? Then from nowhere and from a creature unseen, came the response. A hidden myna bird called back, note for note, mysterious and pure. My father smiled, pleased with himself, and we walked on.

Every time I walked up that hill thereafter, I tried to get that bird to whistle back to me. I whistled, or tried to, but could never quite create the call my father had. There must have been some perfect formation of notes it responded to that someone had taught him. Whatever it was, I couldn't figure it out. I don't recall ever hearing that song back.

As the youngest of my siblings I was the lucky one. Each has a story to tell about their memories of our father. Each has more of those undercurrent moments that I would never get. So with no real everyday experiences of my father before the divorce, I didn't know what I was missing. I didn't know there was another way. You can't crave candy if you don't know what it tastes like. Some kids got candy every day. But I thought it was unusual to see fathers of other kids at scouting events, tee ball and football games. I thought every boy learned how to play catch with his mom.

Summer visits to his house were both comforting and uncomfortable. I was so glad to see my father and yet the familiarity he had with his new family made me feel like an outsider. I loved them, but I couldn't wait to hit the road and have my father to myself for just a little while. He loved to fish, loved to camp and hike and be in nature. In our brief times together, he introduced me to this world, a world I'd never seen before. And it stuck.

Once my father discovered that we shared a love of the outdoors, he did his best to teach me all he knew of these things in our brief visits. Perhaps it was the first time he felt an innate connection to his son. I know it was the first time his son felt that connection with him. It's these moments in our shared passion that are most vivid. How to pitch a tent, start a campfire, tie a fishing knot or dress a freshly caught trout. He taught me how to be at peace in nature. And in those times I was most at peace with him.

In the silence of our long drives through the California back country I'd wonder who this man in the driver's seat was. I'd wonder what he knew about me. He didn't know my friends, or about the kid picking on me at school; or about the girl I had a silent crush on. He had no idea that I felt like I was pretending to be a teenager nor how much I hated school because I felt so alone. He knew none of these things because I would never dare tell him. I could never open up to him because I knew that soon the father would disappear and the stranger return.

We would search for that perfect spot in the middle of a Sierra Nevada lake trawling in a boat or upon its shore. Or better yet a stream. We'd drive without a plan or a map along some road paralleling a mountain spring searching by feel for just the right place to stop. There was no method to it. Just gut. And whimsy. Go until something inside said, "Here! Stop here!" After finding a place to park, we'd have a look around for I know not what. I'd just follow his lead. He'd ask if I thought this was a good place, and I'd nod and say something like, "Looks good." And he'd say, "Good? I think it's better than that. I think this is going to be the best fishing spot yet. Don't you?" And I would fervently agree.

We'd look around to make sure no one else was already there, that no one was nearby to see where we'd gone. It would be our fishing hole and ours alone. Push through the trees and forest to an opening that cradled a tranquil pool along the stream, bordered by a waterfall or rapids above and below, cut off from the rest of the world. It was here we'd stay for hours and hours, content to listen to the river's song even if we weren't catching fish.

But when we did, when we hooked a rainbow trout and pulled it from the cold waters, there was nothing better. That's when I felt like a son. That's when I knew what it was like to have a father. His joy at seeing me pull a fish from the river was so honest and so warm, something I didn't know existed. Fatherly pride. He loved catching fish, but he was so much happier when he saw me do it. I could live in those moments, in that delicious, smothering feeling forever. But they were always over too soon.

By my late teens the contractual visits expired. Though I know he enjoyed our fishing trips, he was no longer required to take me on vacation. We saw each other less and less as his time was focused on trying to be a father to his second family. There would be long stretches with no contact. But I now knew he was out there some-where, and I thought of him from time to time.

I remember a day when I was about twenty and going through a rebellious stage — minor by most standards. I'd just been kicked out of junior college on academic probation and was heading out of the house with an ice chest full a beer to go party with friends. As I was almost out the door, my mother stopped me. She knew where I was going and what I was going to do. She questioned my responsibility, asked when I was going to get serious about school and life. I was still hiding my expulsion from her at this point, so this is a tribute to her maternal instincts.

And in a rare, lucid, if not selfish, burst of masculinity, I said this: "When I'm doing it for me and not you."

She froze and her face stiffened. I'd never seen her look this way before. Stern, yet wounded. And after a weighty silence she replied, "You sound just like your father when you say that."

I was dumbfounded. I had no idea I was anything like him. Absolutely no idea. Though this certainly was not a compliment, it gave me some sense of pride, though that is not the right word. He wasn't the ideal father to be sure, not someone to set the standards by. But this was a genetic straw I could grab; it gave me a feeling of identity, of discovering who I was. A starting point.

So I walked out the door and drank beer with my friends.

I started to see it too, in the way I stood or hooked my finger in my belt. I heard his voice in mine when I laughed or became angry. I had cravings for smoked oysters on a Ritz cracker with a little mayo — his favorite camping appetizer.

And at some point in these years, with my newfound independence and growing sense of self, I made the first efforts to recon-nect with the man outside of my youthful court mandated visits. It started with a casual phone call for no real reason, just catching up. The occasional letter. The children in his second marriage were growing and demanded less of his time now. He'd call to say he was going to be in town for a couple nights and we should have dinner. Besides his love of nature and fishing, I also inherited his infatua-tion with the long, lone road trip. I'd call to tell him I was heading north or east around a certain date and he'd plan to meet me for a couple days in Monterey or Flagstaff. Just the two of us. Again.

As adults, with the labor-intensive efforts of growing up and parenting behind us, we started our relationship anew. A son needs a father. But maybe a father needs a son just as much. It's never too late to tend the old wounds, though they may never be healed.

I could judge him. As a parent now, his mistakes are so much clearer to me. I have moments of reflection when a lonely child's righteous anger wells up within me. These usually come when I'm amazed by my own children and so glad I was present to witness their great triumph or funny dance; to pick them up when they fall and wipe a tear from their cheek. Moments I never had when I was their age.

He's not a perfect father. But I'm far from a perfect son. And we've lost so much time – too many fatherless Father's Days.

When I looked into my two year old's eyes and tried to imagine by what well of self-serving strength I could walk away from her, I felt guilt of such profound depth. It's a pain I'm sure never goes away.

Silent ripples through time. That's what our actions are. That's what happens when we throw a rock into a lake or a river. And we've no idea the myriad ways those boulders will impact us and those around us down the river. His absence in my childhood ripples through my life to this day, but not as much as his presence did and still does.

I'm still that kid whistling into the darkness, and the song I yearn to hear back is one of approval and acceptance from a father. And I'm trying to remember that when I see my children whistling.

There is a river near my house. It starts as a clandestine spring I'll never find atop some far off mountain to the north. On its journey, it cuts through the hearts of cities and people and time. It ends somewhere to the south, past the concrete, in an ocean I can't see from here.

Not yet at least.

Ice Cream Sodas and Buttermilk Donuts

"GRACE like rain falling down on me," the song goes. And sometimes it is like that. But most often with me it's, "Grace like a baseball thrown at the back of my head." Case in point: my 95-year-old grandmother.

Virtually every time my mother has called me over the last few years, I've searched the tone of voice in her first words. The moment she says "Hello," I try to detect whether the next words will be, "Honey, your grandmother died this morning." Every time.

When a call came recently that my grandmother had been losing weight and getting weaker, I did something I've rarely done on my own as an adult. I went to visit my Gammy. She's been slowly withering away in a convalescent home for the last eight years.

She's in the Alzheimer's unit, a locked-down cellblock that prevents the incarcerated from wandering out into the wide-open world of their dementia. I've often wondered whether the security door to the unit was more for their protection or ours.

She sat in her chair watching a television she couldn't see, her eyes cloudy with glaucoma. The nurses keep the televisions on in all the rooms. Somehow the flickering lights and sounds are supposed to breathe life into the scene and make it artificially less heartbreaking.

I knelt down in front of her, gently took her hand, came in close to her ear and screamed, "Hi Grandma! It's Pat!" She hardly moved. Her gaze seemed to outline my silhouette searching for something familiar. Then she mumbled something I took to be a greeting.

Her eyes drifted back toward the television — not really at it but above it, to the corner of the room. An infomercial about home mortgages was on; chatty, energetic snake oil sellers trying to convince her how easy it is to consolidate her debt, improve her credit score and pave the way to financial stability. But I wondered what show or memory or fantasy was playing on that screen she was watching behind those gray eyes.

I sat on the couch beside her chair and simply held her hand. I tried to think of some casual conversation to make. Weather, kids, work, Lindsay Lohan's latest brush with the law. But the situation didn't seem to call for such serious subjects. Instead of idle words, nothing came to my mind. I didn't feel like saying anything. And she seemed agreeable to that.

As I held her hand in mine and caressed it, her body appeared to wilt and relax. With that a recent sermon came to mind. I feel so embarrassingly Christian when that happens. I picture Jesus and my pastor high-fiving each other, thrilled that something finally sunk in. It's a frustrating feeling for someone who hates to admit when others are right.

We were exhorted to "comfort the fainthearted and uphold the weak." Comfort meaning to "come alongside," and uphold meaning to "physically touch." Simple enough.

So we sat in silence holding hands, and I looked into her eyes searching for something, for someone. I wanted to see that person I used to know. What I saw were ice cream sodas and buttermilk doughnuts.

She was a surly old curmudgeon, prone to scowling and grumbling. In our family my Gammy will always be remembered for her crankiness and temper, not her warmth and gregariousness. That legacy of being a loving and warm person will be my mother's, her daughter. It's odd that it turned out this way. Or perhaps not.

But my Gammy and I always got along just fine. I'm not sure why. In my early teens I spent many Friday nights with her. We'd go to a coffee shop for an early-bird dinner and then a movie. After the movie she'd take me out for an ice cream soda. She taught me how to order an ice cream soda properly. Chocolate syrup first, then the seltzer water. One scoop each of vanilla and chocolate ice cream, and a little more seltzer. This made for the perfect combination of rich chocolate, creamy vanilla, carbonation and sweetness. We'd sit in the parlor and enjoy those sodas in mutual, contented silence.

I'd often stay the night at her apartment with its scenic view overlooking the city. In the morning, we'd get buttermilk donuts.

To a kid, the buttermilk donut is not the most attractive of pastries. But I trusted her advice on this and never regretted it.

In hindsight this all seems quite embarrassing: a 14-year-old boy hanging out with his grandmother on a Friday night. And perhaps it was. But at the time I didn't think about it. Peer pressure would soon take me away to hang out with friends. But for those nights, it was just me and Gammy. I felt such a simple joy in having her to myself. It made me feel special.

Her small hands were once strong and sturdy. Now I'm afraid to squeeze them too hard. This fragile, emaciated body is dying. The skin drapes loosely over her skeleton, her eyes are sunken into her skull; her hair thin, wispy and colorless; her fingernails cracked and yellow. She was never a large person, but she was never this small.

I was struck by the overpowering feeling of how sacred and holy it is to be close to someone so near death. I think God likes us to ask the hard questions. So I do wonder why a loving God would allow his children to suffer such a state.

I began to feel so sorry for her, the person trapped in this body. I closed my eyes, laid my hands upon her and prayed that she would be reunited with my grandfather, the center of her life until he died more than 30 years ago. Had she her way, she probably would have gone with him back then. Maybe that's why she was so bitter all these years. She missed her bus in 1975 and saw her love waving at her from the backseat as he drove off to a better place.

I leaned in close and said quietly, "I love you." She turned her gaze to me, and there I saw it. There, somewhere deep in the wrinkles of her paper-thin skin was that old crone smile. My Gammy was in there somewhere, smiling.

She mumbled a faint response back, faint and barely discernable. It sounded like, "You too." Or maybe it was "Yankee doodle." Either way, it made me feel special again.

As I walked down the hall wondering if this would be the last time I saw her alive, I sensed Jesus and my pastor following me. They were geeky and excited. Jesus had a baseball in his hand ready to throw.

I pushed the unit door open and an alarm blared, alerting the staff that someone was trying to escape.

As I waited for an attendant to come help me, I felt vulnerable, scared and exposed. Not to mention embarrassed. I wanted to go back down the hall and hold my Gammy's hand again, to feel safe and comforted by someone who loved me.

The ball bounced off the back of my head and rolled down the hall.

Perhaps God puts these people, in this condition, in our lives to comfort and uphold us, the ones still so vested in this world. Their silence may have something to teach us about ourselves when words fall short. They are not the fainthearted and weak. We are.

The final call did come not too long after, and my Gammy is gone. But she left me with a great view, over the city and my life. It's not about what you see when you look at other people, but what you see them with.

February 21, 2009

❧

A Mother's Work is Never Done

WHILE I'd love to tell the story of your mother today, I don't know her. So, let me tell you about mine. She's a pretty typical mom.

Darlene is a wife, a career educator, a retiree, a volunteer and the epitome of a grandmother. But most of all, she is a mother. A "mom" in the truest sense of the word.

The only child to Cecil and Wilhemina, Darlene was born in the Depression and raised during World War II by parents who made sure their daughter would have more than they did. They sent her off to college, because they never had the opportunity for themselves. She studied to become a teacher, the only job she ever wanted. As expected, she fell in love, got married, began having children and supported her husband as he went from the Air Force to medical school to practicing surgeon. This was the story of so many in her generation.

But times change.

With four children at home ages 2 to 12, her husband left her and the kids. When life deals you a blow like that, you've got to choose between folding or moving on; between the lifelong stain of bitterness or the hopeful optimism in knowing that all things will work out right in the end. Thankfully she chose the latter.

On the modest salary of an elementary school teacher she was able to buy her own home in the hills of Glendale.

Her job allowed her the time to be there as much as possible for her kids, delivering them to three different schools and sundry other activities each day; making sure they had a good dinner on the table every night. Being present is the one great thing any parent can do for their children.

Darlene would remarry a good man, a stable and caring man. He brought with him three kids of his own. Family portraits on the walls of their home display a smiling group clad in polyester and huge lapels and even bigger beehive hair so ubiquitous in the 1970s.

Certainly there were smiles and good times for this extended family. But "The Brady Bunch" it was not.

In the early years of her second marriage, Darlene's doting father, her hero, would be taken from her by cancer at the age of 68, far too young. He was her rock and perhaps the sole reason she has the tender heart she does. Even today when she talks about him, this woman in her 70s becomes a little girl all over again. Her eyes light up and her face beams with a child's smile when she talks about her daddy.

Not long after her father died, Darlene herself would be stricken with cancer. And again, there was a choice to be made. I recall visiting her in the hospital the day of her diagnosis. She was surrounded by lady friends, and she was crying.

Yet through those fearful tears she was laughing, leading the joviality for all in the room with an "oh hell, now this!" attitude. Like she'd caught a cold just before she was supposed to go on vacation.

And then there are the kids. If being a parent, as they say, is taking one's own heart out of your body and placing it in another person, Darlene should be on life support.

The list of her children's transgressions is long. Far too many late-night calls that chill your blood before you've even answered the phone. Totaled cars and more legal issues than she'd care to remember; emergency room visits to sew up bleeding skulls and set broken limbs. School discipline issues, dropouts and runaways; mental illnesses and disorders. Divorce, drug abuse, alcoholism, dependency and co-dependency. She's seen her children and stepchildren battle addiction, demons, depression and one another. She's seen them become prodigals, paupers and widows.

Yet, she put her head down and got through each and every trial focused to do one thing: get to tomorrow. Divorce: get to tomorrow. Cancer: get to tomorrow. Addiction: get to tomorrow. Death: get to tomorrow.

A mother lives through her children, aching and suffering for them as they go through their struggles, wishing she could take those burdens upon herself.

She watches helplessly as her own heart takes beating after beating, knowing better but unable to magically solve the problems her children create for themselves. I imagine it's a bit how God feels for us.

We grew up near a golf course in Glendale, California. As kids it was our playground. I drove by it recently and saw an enormous excavation of the underground reservoir beneath it. The grass had been torn off to reveal the concrete and rebar structures underneath the fairways and greens. We always knew there was a reservoir under there, but it was off limits; a forbidding and dark place we were too fearful or ignorant to explore.

Reflecting on childhood from the vantage point of time has a way of doing that — tearing the surface off, exposing what lies beneath.

It can be shocking to see the rawness, the nakedness of the things hidden from our view, shattering one's own created image of what one thinks is real.

I thought I had a perfectly normal childhood. And I was right.

As children we don't know what was suffered on our behalf. And this is the testimony of a mother.

She protects us from the fearful and forbidding things in life.

She may not catch us every time we fall, but she covers us in ways we never knew. She tells you everything is going to be all right even when she herself doesn't know if it will. And we trust her.

Happy Mother's Day, from all your sons and daughters. And thank you.

May 9, 2009

Boys and Barbershops

SO I'M driving home the other day, and we pass a barber shop. The kids notice the candy stick-like barber pole out front and ask what that means.

"I'm glad you ask," I tell them, and proceed to enlighten them with what Wikipedia told me.

"In the Middle Ages," I start, "barbers not only cut hair, but also performed surgery and tooth extractions. Oh, and they used leeches for bloodletting. A basin at the top of the pole represented the vessel in which the leeches were kept. A basin at the bottom of the pole represented the vessel that received the spilled blood. The pole itself represents the staff that the patients gripped for dear life during their procedures. The white stripes represent clean bandages and the red stripes represent, well you guessed it, blood stained ones."

The kids don't ask me these kinds of questions anymore, and I now sleep on the couch.

When I sit in my barber's chair, invariably, the first thing he asks me is this:

"The usual abbreviation?"

This kind of familiarity is something I think most men seek. It's what makes us love our bartenders and is the same mysterious force that compels us to buy five of the same shirts when we find one we like.

Drive up Riverside Drive in Toluca Lake, just past the Trader Joe's, and you'll see the trademark red, white and blue spinning pole. An enormous sign announces, "Barber Shop." It's called Shear Pleasure, but don't let the name fool you. This is a barber shop in the truest sense.

The place smells of hair tonic and musk and shoe polish, scents from a bygone era. They sell male grooming products that haven't been purchased since Johnson was in the White House. There are TVs on the wall, big band music playing in the background and a guy that'll shine your shoes for just a couple bucks. It's clean, friendly and everyone's a regular.

John's my barber and he's been cutting hair for almost 50 years. He doesn't ask me what conditioner I'd like, nor does he recommend a fabulous new deep hydrating volumizer treatment. I get my best dirty jokes from John, though I don't think I've ever repeated one. I am regaled by his raspy wit while he takes a No. 4 razor to my mop. For 20 peaceful minutes, I am taken back to my childhood.

When I was a kid in Glendale in the 1970s there was only one place to get your haircut — Ernie's Barber Shop. It's been at the same location, run by the same man, for more than 60 years.

Ernie's was where a young man got his hair cut. And you had your hair cut by barbers, not hair stylists or cosmetologists. For a boy growing up anywhere in the vicinity of Chevy Chase Drive and Glenoaks Boulevard, Ernie's was a rite of passage.

Though I am sure my memory is skewed by the veil of time, when I think back to Ernie's Barber Shop, I think of a simpler era. A time before cell phones and the Internet, before political correctness and gender blending, before metrosexuality and man-scaping.

I recall being dropped off at Ernie's after school while my mother ran errands. We boys sat and waited our turn, unknowingly absorbing the air of masculinity around us; listening with burning ears and dropped jaws to the ribbing and joking and male-speak of the barbers. It was the kind of good-natured jawing that would prepare us for locker rooms, barrooms and poker tables in the years to come.

When we finally got in the chair, we did what we were told. Lift your head, sit still, don't slouch. Often your brother or a friend from school would do their best to make you laugh or move, hoping for blood or just a missed snip. But their turn would come soon.

Ernie's was the kind of place that young, impressionable men discovered the exquisite beauty of the female form. Or at least this young man did. It was during one of those visits at the age of eight when my mother had dropped me off that I opened my first Playboy magazine while I waited my turn. If any of the barbers saw me sneaking this peak, they turned a blind eye.

The incident has become one of those stories told regularly at my family gatherings, how I cried for days when my mother refused to get me my own subscription. For years after this, I was determined to one day become a Playboy photographer.

If this all sounds nostalgic and dreamy, perhaps it is. Maybe it was just another barber shop, nothing special. But I believe that when people do something right, and do that something right for so long, they become a patch in the fabric of life, connecting so many other lives.

A boy never looks forward to a haircut in the way young ladies must look forward to visits to the beauty salon. But somehow it was easier to take when you knew you'd be going to Ernie's.

I don't recall ever getting a balloon or a lollipop after a haircut. I never did become a photographer for Playboy, and I plead the 5th as to whether I ever got my own subscription. But I do believe that I, and most boys who went through the rite of passage that is Ernie's, got so much more.

May 30, 2009

❧

What to Do After You Say 'I Do'

WHAT would you tell two starry-eyed people about to embark on the rosy path of marriage?

My brother and his fiancée asked me to give a "short" speech on marriage at their wedding. I told them there is no such thing. A short speech on marriage is like a "quick trip" to the summit of Mt. Everest.

After seriously questioning their judgment and their choice of people to turn to for advice, I tried to think of anything I've learned in my happy marriage that I could offer them. Here is what I came up with and am telling them today.

First and foremost, be friends. In tough times, you'll need to return to the safety and security of that friendship to see you through. And in good times, well, in good times you get to be "friends with privileges."

Marriage is about the long, slow journey; the moments, simple daily moments. Lively bedroom conversations lasting deep into the night; long, speechless road trips through the desert. The time she threw out her back and was paralyzed with pain so you caught the first flight back from a business trip in Las Vegas. Or when you gave her bad directions and got her lost for hours in the dark woods late at night on that family vacation. These are the moments that make up a path stretching far into a future you can't see or imagine.

Strive for trust and stability, not excitement and adventure. That's not to say you won't have the latter. You will. But adventure and excitement are the reward you get for first achieving trust and stability.

Marriage is about letting each other do the things that drive the other person crazy. Don't argue over the little things, like how she lets knives dry in the drying rack tips up; or how much you hate that old, worn out pair of pants he's owned for 15 years. When he tells you the same story for the 50th time, and each time it's gotten more fanciful, smile, nod and tell him what a great story it is. There are just some things men and women will never understand about each other.

Rather than trying to change each other, learn to love each other for exactly who you each are. Be honest with each other, even if it hurts. Marriage is about allowing someone to hurt you and still loving them; it's about hurting them back and finding they still love you. Let that person tell you everything that is wrong with you, all the things you already knew but could never face alone.

Argue. Challenge each other. Push each other to do good and be better. Know that the baggage and issues you each bring into this partnership don't magically disappear on your wedding day. In fact, they may intensify. Be prepared to battle not only your own demons in the years to come, but each other's.

You are allowed to freak out at any time, and in fact it's encouraged. But not at the same time. One of you always has to be the safe harbor, the one who says, "Get over it!" or "There, there, everything will be all right," even when you don't know if it will.

Laugh. Laugh as much as possible, at yourself and each other. But always laugh at yourself first. It's unfair and unkind to laugh at others if you haven't first proven yourself to be an equal or greater fool.

Find your balance with each other. To use a sports analogy, you need a starting pitcher and a closer. My wife knows that it may take me years to start a household project. But if she starts it — painting a room or tearing up the carpet in the entire house — I can't help but jump in to see it through. If she doesn't do her part, the job will never get done. If I don't do mine, it will never get done... right.

A rough road lies ahead. Arguments, money struggles, interior decorating decisions, filing jointly. But something even more wonderful is about to come your way: Routine. Stability. Knowing. And at last comfort. A comfort you've never known was possible. A comfort that allows you to be your sloppy, world weary, beaten down and annoying self; the person behind the façade who said you had everything under control.

Stop caring about the things the rest of the world cares about — image, income, new toys, Jon and Kate, Michael Jackson's kids or what Paula Abdul is going to do now. Don't compare yourself to any other couples you know. Focus solely on each other.

Long after the honeymoon, take time each day to remember the feeling that brought you here today — that magical sense of knowing that this was the person you've been waiting for all these years. The feeling that isolated you two from the rest of the world and made you pity everyone else, for surely no one else has ever felt like this before. Keep that feeling for yourselves like a firefly in a jar and put it up on your dresser. Bring it down at least once each day, open it up for a moment and remember.

As I was putting these thoughts down on paper, I received an e-mail from my brother, and he said this:

"Yesterday was a long day. Woke up early, went to work, got home, cooked dinner, unpacked boxes in the new house, put beds together, collapsed into bed. This could have been any long day, with the exception that I was collapsing next to her. We didn't say anything to each other; we were too tired. She simply put her hand on my back as we fell asleep together. It was the warmest, most reassuring hand I've ever felt."

And with that I realized there was nothing more I could say.

August 15, 2009

ᕦᐁᕤ

Leaving Comfort Zone

I WAS feeling rather morose the other day. Kind of pathetic, lowly, defeated and self loathing. There was a dull pain in my chest that I attribute to being unsatisfied with my job, having not left a significant mark upon this world by the age of 42, having neither made the best seller list — which would actually require writing a book — nor being a millionaire and owning a vacation home in either Cambria or Palm Springs. Or it could be the high cholesterol.

I needed to get myself out of this funk. Sometimes we have to do something physical to trigger something emotional and spiritual.

I started looking for something to write about, forcing myself really, and opened an old journal I'd written in 1994 while on a road trip through the Four Corners region of the southwest.

Not long ago I read that the Four Corners marker is not actually in the right place. The cement block famed for being the exact location where the corners of Arizona, Colorado, New Mexico and Utah meet is in fact 1,875 feet away from the real geographical location, experts say. Placing too much faith in the manmade can be a mistake.

I recognize the words in this journal and the person who wrote them, and I am embarrassed for him. He was young, so young in so many ways — single and without responsibilities. His words are the rhapsodic ramblings of an adventure-seeking dreamer. And he's scared to death when he finds it.

With the classical music of Corelli blaring on the tape deck, I'd left Flagstaff, Ariz., and drove through Monument Valley into the remotest regions of southern Utah. As day's end neared, I followed a line on a map that was supposed to lead me to a small town. The paved road turned to dirt, and the dirt to mud as an ominous rain began to fall. And what I found in place of civilization was an abandoned motel and several acres of junked cars.

I turned back, needle on empty, and retraced my route. It was at least 50 miles in any direction to any dot on the map, not that I trusted the map anymore. The words in this journal entry are that of a scared, lost, intimidated and humbled fool; lost in the wilderness I'd put myself in, about to stall out on a dirt road and overcome with panic at being alone in the wilds of Utah.

I haven't changed much in 15 years.

I have days when I feel like a competent parent; never a great one, just coping and not making too many mistakes. Those are the good days. Most of the time I feel like fodder for my daughters' tell-all book 30 years from now; a lazier, heavier version of Joan Crawford in "Mommy Dearest."

I go to church, but often forget to take it with me. I am an employee, but would rather not be in the office. I am a son, but haven't said thank you enough to my parents. I am a citizen, but water my lawn more than recommended. I am a cook, but don't feed enough people. I am a human, but am too often inhumane.

I am not a man of action. Never have been. I'm one who lets life unfold before him rather than wrenching it open myself. And while I'm letting the world happen, I'm constantly distracted — by work, chores, tabloid headlines and Discovery Channel shows about fish or bridges. All of the things we fill our time with, the things that keep our minds occupied so we can't hear the silence or feel the real emotions inside that scare us. We're so distracted we neglect to see that the needle is on empty.

What we need to do once in a while is put ourselves 50 or 1,000 miles out of our comfort zone down a dirt road and see what happens. We need self discovery, not just the "looking inward" kind, but the looking outward at the world kind. Make things out there known in here, in yourself. The Grand Canyon is just a myth until you see it for yourself. And so is happiness.

Ever notice how you feel a little more at peace with yourself when you wear your favorite shirt? How your car seems to drive better after you've washed it? How much more you appreciate life after you've jumped out of a plane and the parachute opens?

It's communion. Taking a cracker and imparting it with the power to change you. A physical action symbolizing a spiritual benchmark. An expression of faith in something outside yourself, for we can't do it on our own.

You don't have to walk on hot coals, but there's nothing wrong with that. Maybe all you need is a new haircut.

As my car sputtered into a campsite that wasn't on the map, I came across a park ranger named Nate. I about cried. He told me he could only sell me four gallons of gas; more than I needed. I took his gas, but stayed the night in his beautiful hidden campground. I can still picture the southwest sky catching fire as the sun set after the rains.

I've been thinking a lot lately about change. And it scares the hell out of me. It's an understandable fear, but it paralyzes me with inaction nonetheless.

At some point I have to learn that I'm not in control. Nate is.

August 29, 2009

❧

Legends of the Fall and Nepal

AS DIFFERENT as people and traditions are around the world, sometimes it's the similarities that sneak up on us and surprise us the most.

For three days and three nights I'd been stuck in this village, a day's hike from the airfield, a week away from Kathmandu and ages from home.

Centuries old, Dunai sits at the crossroads of several primary trekking routes in the lower Dolpo region of Nepal, a frontier land reachable only by plane. The only highways are dirt roads, the only traffic infrequent trekkers, beastly yaks and brilliantly ordained cows. The freezing, jade-hued glacial waters of the Bheri River carve this deeply cut Himalayan valley, and I cannot leave here until my Sherpa feels the autumn weather is right for us to move on.

I'm the only Westerner staying at our lodge, the Blue Sheep Hotel. Though the accommodations are far too rustic to really be considered a hotel, it's the nicest place I'll see for weeks to come. I may be the only Westerner in the entire village, actually. Or at least that's what it feels like as I walk through the town's cobblestoned streets. Never have I felt so alone among so many people.

Tall, white, blond hair, blue eyes. I stand out among the ruddy, Mongol-Aryan villagers with their earthen skin and straight, coal-black hair. Casual strolls to consume idle time become awkward as every eye locks upon me, the unknown and exotic stranger in a place where the unfamiliar becomes a spectacle and reason for crowds to come running.

I'd become so uncomfortable with the gawking attention of the villagers, I spent most of my time sequestered within the compound of the lodge. On this, the first sunny afternoon since I'd arrived, I took a chair from the dining hall and sat outside trying to while away the enemy time by enjoying a book or writing in my journal.

In the Himalayas, time is tracked not on a clock, but by how far you can walk in a day and by watching the sun cast a crawling shadow upon the sheer mountain walls. The escaping light bounces off the bronze-colored canyon and powdery clouds overhead, changing the landscape minute by minute. Blink and you're looking at a new painting of the same scene, like Van Gogh's haystacks.

Not long after settling in, as if on cue, a group of children, maybe 20 in all, ages 2 to 15, entered the courtyard. Some I recognized from the village — kids that had followed me wherever

I went. They acknowledged me in their humble, shy Nepali way. Each was wearing what was surely their finest clothing: semi-clean collared shirts and thick woolen trousers not yet frayed at the hem. Yet most were still barefoot. All had a fresh red tika painted on their forehead.

One boy, about 10, tapped out a soft, consistent rhythm on a simple drum strapped over his shoulder. The children formed into a circle in the middle of the courtyard. They began to hum and chant, solemn and cheerful. Then one boy began to sing alone in words I couldn't understand. He was bashful and sang through the collar of his shirt, which he held over his mouth. After each verse the others repeated him.

Their eyes would look at me, then dart away each time I made eye contact. A crowd of villagers gathered around to watch, smiling the way grown-ups do when children put on a show in the living room.

Then a girl no older than seven began to sing. But she was not so shy. Her melodic voice echoed off the adobe walls, carrying out and beyond the lodge, beckoning even more villagers to come. I was glad I couldn't understand the lyrics. Her fearless voice alone transcended language, saying more than I could ever comprehend in words.

Then the singers dispersed and, still singing, walked around the courtyard approaching the gathered audience. People handed the children coins, then lifted their clasped hands to their forehead and bid them, "Namaste." A few of the more bold singers approached me, so I dug into my pocket and handed out rupees to each who asked.

Their concert complete, the young choir exited the courtyard, walked up the trail and out of sight. Several looked back to get one more shy glance at the stranger from far away.

My questioning and frustration at being stuck in this village for three days had finally been answered.

One of the lodge workers, a friendly man who spoke serviceable English, told me this was the first day of an annual fall festival. On this day groups of children dressed up and went from house to house singing in this way, receiving alms from grown-ups.

As I went to record all this in my journal, I saw that the day's date was October 31.

I think of these kids each Halloween when I follow my costumed children and their friends from door to door as they bravely and shyly ask for sweet offerings. Maybe I can get them to sing this year.

October 31, 2009

⚜

Losing My Job, Losing Control

THE day you get fired usually starts like any other. But it sure ends differently.

When I'm not waxing rhapsodic in this column each week, I work in the entertainment industry full time. Or at least I did. Until two weeks ago.

After overseeing the layoff of several colleagues, hearing things like "economic downturn," "declining revenues" and "difficult cutbacks" repeated to each, I moved from one side of the table to the other. Terminator to terminatee.

Times have been hard, so it was somewhat expected, as were the placating closing words: "It has nothing to do with your performance. As soon as things turn around you'll be the first one called back. Stay in touch, and let us know if you need a recommendation." Yeah, I've said those words too.

So home I went to begin the seven stages of job loss grief: Denial, Anger, Bargaining, Beer, Tequila, Häagen Dazs, Acceptance. I'm much better now.

I was laid off once before, and to be honest, it was one of the best things that ever happened to me. Freelancing to make ends meet gave me a new appreciation for employers. Belt tightening is always a good lesson. And I lost 15 pounds.

Since then I've grown irritated with my employer, bought exercise equipment that collected more dust than I did muscle, and I gained 20 pounds.

As well as joining many friends and acquaintances in the ranks of the laid off, I am also now a member of the alarming 12% in the workforce who are unemployed. And while they say the economy is turning around, they also say California will be at the tail end of that turnaround.

I'm not unlike millions of people in any other field. You work hard, think you're safe, commit yourself to a company for years hoping someday it succeeds and the profits at the top will trickle down to those working so hard in the trenches. Then you find that in business there is no such thing as true security. In the hands of men, there are no Golden Rules when money is involved.

I don't know about you, but I'm not good when I find I'm not really in control of my life. I panic with the same shock I get when I'm sick and find my body doing nasty things I can't stop by sheer willpower.

Maybe it's just a lesson I need to learn, which is why I repeat it so much. But I am not in control. And looking back at my life, I wonder if I've ever been.

Sure, I've made life-changing decisions, chosen which classes, jobs and roads to take. But life is a dark country highway, and you can see only as far ahead as your headlights shine. What's beyond that is as unknown and unstable as Britney Spears on a bender.

When you measure your life, think whether the great things in it came through your own strangling, paranoid control, your desperate faith to your own brilliance, insight and lifelong series of perfect decisions. Or rather, has luck, providence, coincidence or an "act of God" ever shifted the tectonic plates under your feet, sending you spiraling in a new trajectory not of your will?

All that we desperately cling to in our belief that we are the masters of our own destiny can be taken away so easily. And I'm not just talking about a job.

All that is good and wonderful and true in life comes to us through grace, a gift given without instigation or condition:

The chance encounter, which led to a kiss, which led to a wedding and a new life together.

A call from a friend just when the world felt like a yawning grave, and all you needed was a caring hand to hold for a moment.

When two microscopic cells miraculously find their way to each other, combine, multiply into complex new forms and become life itself.

It's so hard for us to understand this: that we control none of it. And when we forget, when we get complacent, stagnant or too comfortable with ourselves, we need to have things shaken up. If we don't do it for ourselves, it will be done for us.

It's grace, like rain, like a shower. And in a society that tells us rain is "bad" weather, we ignore the healing and change it brings. This didn't happen to me, or to you, as punishment. It happened to cleanse us, to prepare us for new growth.

I know it's scary. I know money doesn't grow on trees. But I can't control that either. So what do we do?

We hold our heads high; knock on doors to see which open. If they don't open, we move on. If they do open, go in and see if that room's decorated for you. We help others because we end up helping ourselves more than them. We look around and appreciate all of the marvelous things we've missed while behind a desk in a fluorescent-hued office, for we may be back there sooner than we want.

Be strong and courageous. Do not be frightened or dismayed. Have faith.

November 7, 2009

❦

Only the Dust Remains

EARTH to earth. Ashes to ashes. And dust to dust.

Last week, before the rains came, I was driving south down the 5 Freeway on one of those clear, windy SoCal days when everything is glare and static. I'd just spent the morning visiting my father. We like to get together for breakfast, eat sausage, bacon and biscuits with gravy. The things we know we're not supposed to eat.

And we drink coffee. Lots of it. He likes to take me to new places, out-of-the-way diners and roadhouses where we get stared at by the regulars and every waitress is named Flo or Jean.

We jaw like long lost friends, which we are. And like old friends, there's a comfort in our times together. But also wounds. I am reminded each time of the great healing power of family bonds, as well as the equally destructive power when those bonds are broken. And as I drive home, my thoughts turn to the lasting, unforeseen repercussions of events so long ago. The remains.

Then I see it. High above, over the hills to the east.

Clouds of it. Swarms.

Where in August there were great columns of smoke and ash in our hills, there are now rolling torrents of dust. The stripped-bare land giving rise to the air what it has left. What remains.

A humble offering. A silent reminder.

Dust.

It seems so far away in the distance, out there. But I look away, lost in a moment's reflection of fire and trial, pain and suffering. And when I look back it's gone. I think it's disappeared. But it hasn't. I've driven into the cloud, and it surrounds me; the dust is a pall over us that we have trouble seeing when we're shrouded in it. But it is there. Always.

I get home, turn on the TV and witness the devastation in Port-au-Prince. The earth shifts violently beneath our feet, and everything collapses; lives are taken and destroyed. The images are surreal and almost unwatchable. And after the shaking stops, there is silence and dust. A cloud over their land, the reports all say. And then the screaming starts. Toppled buildings and bodies are what remain; passing memorials to sudden destruction.

Dust.

A veil over our hills, our homes, over our cars, our streets, our land and lives. Born of fire and fuel, of sudden movements of earth. It is the afterthought we try not to think about. Dust is what remains. And it always returns. Whether borne on the wind in great masses over our heads, in sheets upon our belongings or mixed with rainwater flooding the ground at our feet. The dust always returns.

It's a nuisance, a bother. Something we don't want to deal with or ask others to deal with for us. It's a reminder of loss, damage and decay, of passing time we won't get back, made worse when brought upon ourselves by our own actions.

Destruction comes blindly in so many forms. A child's wailing cry from the depths of crushing concrete and steel; from the other room as a mother tries to wish the hate away. Violence and abuse. Anger. Envy, lust, greed. Abandonment. Selfish devotions. Tomorrow, maybe tomorrow. I promise. Silence. Unspoken suffering. Fatherless sons, motherless daughters. Divorce, hatred, spite. Regret.

It's all fire. It's all earth-shattering.

And what remains, days, months, years later, is dust. Wash it away with a leaf blower, garden hose or another pill; sweep it under that lovely new rug. It obeys. Briefly.

But look up, up to those hills that have known us so long, have seen more than time; hills that have cast their shadows over us since creation. They know.

Dust, carried on tides of wind, currents of time. Fight back the tide and feel the sand give way under your feet. Like oceans the tide of dust flows and ebbs with the rhythm of our world. Pulled by a moon so far away, and by a gravity that grounds us. Unseen forces, but we know they are there.

Look back over your life and count the destruction; survey the remains of what you've done and what has been done to you.

Tides of dust that speak no words, yet scream in the quiet: I won't go away. I am both cause and effect. I am what remains of your actions and of all destruction. Not evil, but not kind either. Simply present. Eternal echoes. And I've but one question for you: What will you do with me?

Rinse me away? Embrace me? Accept, learn, grow? Ignore? Rebuild?

Forgive?

Dust.

From it we are made. To it we return. Over and over again. The curse of our own doing. And yet, also our hope.

January 23, 2010

Still a Lot to Learn at School

"Pat needs to increase his efforts in oral participation... He needs to place more emphasis on neatness rather than hurrying through his work...He did not work as hard as he should have in several areas." — comments on my sixth-grade report card.

AND as true today as when Mrs. Grossman wrote them 31 years ago.

In a world where few people stay with the same employer for more than a few years, Mrs. Grossman is an anomaly. She told me her first name is Barbara, but I refuse to believe that elementary school teachers have first names.

Her first teaching job was at Glenoaks Elementary School, and that is where I found her one recent rainy day, in the same classroom, 38 years later. As I sat in my old classroom — taking in the smell of damp leaves, wet kid and eraser dust — the memories came flooding back. It helped that the desks were the same ones I sat in back then — someone please remind me where that California Lottery money is supposed to go.

But mostly it was this woman, my teacher, the unchanging face of my school days.

From the eyes of a child, teachers don't so much seem old as ageless. Ask them how old their teacher is, and they'll have no idea. But I never expected Mrs. Grossman to be so youthful, more so today than when I sat in her class. Maybe being around children so long has something to do with it.

"It's still neat to come to work here," she told me. "I can't think of anything else I'd rather be doing."

Another rarity for workers of any kind.

My visit was not without motive, I had to admit. I've been harboring a dark secret for 31 years.

Back then, Mrs. Grossman held a reading competition called the "Room 15 500." On a bulletin board was a racetrack sectioned like a game board. For every book you read, you moved your race car ahead one space. While other kids advanced their cars 15, 20, 25 books, I remained dead last. Two books. And then the admission:

"I didn't even read those books, Mrs. Grossman." I was 11 years old again, ashamed and in trouble. She looked at me with the wizened, gentle authority that all good teachers have.

"Well, you might have been just as honest as the child who claimed to read 15 or 30."

I exhaled in relief, thus assured she wouldn't revoke my passing grade, and my entire educational career wouldn't come crashing down like a house of cards.

As we looked through old photos and memorabilia, it became clear she remembered every student who came through her door. Former students are now her colleagues. She's taught the children of her former pupils.

But before I could ask her what that feels like, we came across a telling inscription in my yearbook that begged explanation. A girl wrote to me: "Have a great summer. See you next year. P.S. lay off the dirty pictures." And I had to recall a most embarrassing story.

During a science project studying pictures of cell structures, I decided to draw my own pictures. But mine were devoted to the human female form rather than bacteria. Upon seeing my pictures, the class troublemaker grabbed them and showed them to the pretty young lady sitting next to me, much to my squeaky-voiced protests. I was called to show Mrs. Grossman the object of this uproar.

"What would your father think if I showed him this?" she asked sternly.

After giving it serious thought, I answered honestly, "He'd probably laugh."

Mrs. Grossman didn't like this answer. And I never did become a Playboy photographer.

"I wonder what ever happened to him," she said of that troublemaker.

And as we looked through more pictures, she made the same comment about so many kids. When she asked me what my favorite part of her class was, I didn't hesitate: When she read us "The Chronicles of Narnia." The whole class was mesmerized, fearing the end of each chapter and yearning for the next.

Soon something occurred to me. I'd come to interview her. But it was me we ended up talking about; so curious was she about her students and their lives after they left her charge. It must be hard to get so close to kids at such a critical time of their development, then see them off to the purgatory of junior high and life beyond. She hoped against hope that each would survive and succeed, whether they became lawyers, bookkeepers, taxi drivers or doctors.

"One of my fears though," she told me, "is that I'll end up at the hospital needing some procedure and a former student will be the doctor. Can we get somebody else in here?!"

She's seen so much change, in kids, school politics and the educational system. She has air conditioning and better ventilation in her class now, stifling the scent of sweaty boys and asphalt on a hot day. But the heart of a good teacher remains constant. She's in it for the kids. Always has been.

When I asked her what she wanted her students to take away from her class, she said what she's supposed to say first.

"The basics, reading and writing at grade level."

Then she paused and added what is clearly in her heart.

"A sense of kindness."

Teachers are rarely wrong in their assessments of their students.

"Pat needs to increase his efforts and work harder in several areas."

And she's still teaching me how to do that.

February 6, 2010

Through the Wounds

THERE are two things you shouldn't cheap out on: a good pair of shoes and a good tax accountant. I have a good accountant. But when he gives me my results this year, I want to kick him in his "depletable assets" with my Red Wing boots.

"But I'm unemployed," I whimper. "I can't owe."

"Sorry," he shrugs.

Accountants. Good with numbers, bad with words.

On my way home I meet with a friend for lunch. Over onion rings and fried cheese sticks he tells me how he just isn't sure yet where to buy that second house, about his plans on expending his first one and the resurgence of his 401k.

And I think, I had one of those once.

At home I grab the mail. Instead of checks and Happy Ash Wednesday greeting cards, I find bills and a dispassionate letter from the unemployment office notifying me of a required "phone interview."

Hey, at least it's an interview.

So I assume the position. No, not prone on the couch with a bottle of tequila sans glass, though I was tempted.

My fetal position is this: sitting at my desk staring out the window trying to see the sky through the leafless branches of the trees, chewing the inside of my cheek and mindlessly plucking follicles from my already pathetic goatee. This goes on for about 20 minutes. Or five hours. I lose track.

Nutty Boy, our adopted pet squirrel, climbs down from his tree and unearths the almonds I gave him last summer, digging them up from the lawn where he hid them. As he eats one I watch him and he stares back. But I'm in no mood for a staring contest. He always wins anyway.

There goes the family vacation, I'm thinking. I hope the kids don't need new shoes or elective reconstructive surgery this year.

And then I wonder, did I actually see the kids go through the gate at school this morning? I kissed them at the curb, saw them walk towards the gate. But did I actually *witness* them walk *through* the gate? Are they still standing there, crying, lost, eight feet from the entrance, ignored by their teachers and the kindly but distracted yard duty ladies?

What kind of father am I? What kind of husband am I? I'm supposed to be the head of my household, leading my family by example. And now my six-year-old is going to have to postpone that Heidi Montag Surgery Package she's been saving for. The wife will be forced to sell a kidney so we can keep all 300 channels on AT&T U-Verse.

What example am I setting? Sure, they know how to eat Cheetos without smearing orange dust on the TV remote, but in this job market there are guys with Master's Degrees who can do that.

I distract myself perusing the posted horoscopes of friends on Facebook, ignoring their pleas for help in "offing" someone in a Mafia War and wondering where they plan on keeping all the virtual farm animals they've herded.

And a former co-worker, also laid off, pops up in a chat. It's getting hard to find things that still need fixing or cleaning around the house, he tells me. But the family's underwear is washed, the kids are in school and happy. Let's meet for a beer soon. A cheap one.

Something catches my eye outside, not because it's quick or bright. Quite the opposite. It's an old, gray couple, holding hands, shuffling slowly down the street. They stop, catch their breath, look up at Nutty Boy chattering in his tree. She lovingly pats her husband's depletable asset and they move along.

When I taste blood from the inside of my cheek and there's a quarter-sized bald spot on my chin, I stop and close my eyes. I try to clear my mind of everything: the snarky look on the faces of the IRS agents when they get my return, the visions of my children eating free cheese sandwiches in the school cafeteria, the wife coming home at 6 a.m. after pulling a second shift for the third time this week, all of us piled into a leaky inflatable pool in the backyard this summer instead of the swim-up bar at some tropical resort pool.

I push that all out and embrace the dark and the silence. At last.

Then, just piercing the veil, I see the faces of two friends. They're married and have kids close in age to ours. One of them was just laid off. The other got news from the doctor that no one ever wants to get. And they're smiling.

They are smiling.

And I think of one of those things you learn in church that you know is always about someone else, never you: look at the birds of the air and how they don't fret for their next meal.

So I watch Nutty Boy to see where he's hid the other nuts. I'll need to show my girls where to find them.

In a book I'm reading, there's a picture of a Native American rug. The rug has a small imperfection in one corner. It's said this blemish is left there intentionally by the maker. That's where the spirit enters.

Through the wound. Through the pain. Through the suffering. That's where the spirit enters. The spirit of warmth. Of growth. And finally, peace.

Just look at the squirrels of the trees.

And I notice that, though it's only February, small buds are starting to appear on those barren branches outside.

Suffering unites. Love Transcends. Seasons change.

February 27, 2010

❧

Serving Justice Fresh

SITTING at the Burbank Metrolink stop waiting for a train to Union Station on my first day of jury duty, I realize why there are so many cars on the freeway and so few people waiting with me at the station. My Metrolink ticket cost $9. That's right. The equivalent of three gallons of gas.

After a quick stop at Glendale's rustic, mission style station, it's only a few relaxing minutes to downtown Los Angeles. There are few things more peaceful than watching the world pass by from inside a train. Past buildings and rivers of concrete, past rail yards and a cornfield of inedible corn that once was. And graffiti. Graffiti everywhere. Some with artistic merit, but most with none.

17 minutes from Burbank to Union Station, with its high-beamed ceilings and mosaic floors so polished you can see the reflection of fedora-wearing travelers from a bygone era. I make

the short walk to the courthouse and as commutes go, this is one I could get used to.

I was prepared with books, newspapers and my laptop to while away time in the jury room. But, I was immediately called into a jury selection and spent the rest of the day listening to prospective jurors divulge too much personal information about themselves under questioning from the four attorneys in the courtroom. Note to self: admitting to spousal abuse, drunk driving and being the victim of identity theft do not automatically disqualify one from jury service. But a pre-planned upcoming vacation to the Grand Canyon does.

By the end of the day 12 jurors are seated, and I think I'm off the hook. But the court wastes no time in randomly selecting two alternates. Minutes later, while counsel is packing their bags to head home, I'm sworn in as juror number 13. Lucky me. A friend rightly described being an alternate juror like this: all of the pain, none of the glory.

I arrive on Day One ready to serve justice, fresh and with a side of humanity. But all rules of common decency and civility are waived when it comes to riding the elevator in government buildings. There's no holding of the door for the elderly or ladies first. One squeezes in as fast as possible, praying the doors close, the cable holds and you actually stop at the designated floors. Don't look at each other; you may be riding with the witness, lawyer or defendant in the very case you're assigned. Rather, stare at the graffiti etched into the stainless steel walls of the elevator.

The courtroom itself is an austere and solemn place. Like church, the seats are uncomfortable enough to make sure your attention is on the proceedings and not drifting elsewhere. The plain wood-paneled walls appear to lean inwards over you, and every one of the 200 visually toxic fluorescent ceiling lights is working perfectly. The great seal of California hovers over the judge's head, a man strikingly resembling a cross between Harry Anderson from "Night Court" and Ben Stein from "Ferris Buehler's Day Off."

We hear testimony about rival street gangs and a neighborhood caught between them. We're given an education on gang membership, graffiti, signs and tattoos. Police officers describe what they saw and defendants' counsel tries to discredit them, repeatedly finding areas of reasonable doubt. With every new witness or piece of admitted evidence, I think I know the truth. But then the defense argues, and I see their point. After all, I'm coming to learn, it's not about truth, but proof.

On Day Two I arrive to find that one juror has been excused for reasons untold. Like the starting quarterback blowing out a knee, the second string is called in. Good thing I took notes yesterday.

More testimony and arguments; nothing as exciting as "Law and Order" or even "Judge Judy." On breaks, we sit in the stoic halls, defendants and jurors avoid eye contact or sitting on the same bench. It's more awkward than running into an ex while dining out with your spouse. Whether there at their lawyer's behest or not, you can't help but accept that the accused have mothers, fathers, lovers and kids of their own.

When the people and the defense rest, we retire to the bleak jury room. Here, where the water fountain doesn't work and the clock is permanently stuck at 2:37, the full weight of this responsibility becomes evident. 12 average people, supposed peers, must now choose sides. I imagine my kids fighting over a pen and coming to me for justice, not knowing who to believe. In those cases I take the pen away and no one gets it. But I can't do that here.

On the final day, we make our decision and present it to the judge. The verdicts are read, and we the jury in the above entitled action stare hard at the floor, the walls, the ceiling. Anywhere but at the defendants. We try not to comprehend the repercussions beyond what is our now completed duty.

We're released and stream single file out of the courtroom with a nervous, eager pace. And holding the door for us as we exit is a young woman with a small child in her arms, a child I've seen curled up in the defendant's lap during recess in the hall. She holds the door for us, staring at the ground as tears streak her lost face.

And as I ride home to my quiet suburban street, I watch the graffiti pass by outside my train. Plenty of pain and very little glory.

April 3, 2010

The Coming of Summer

REMEMBER when movies started with the lights dimming and the curtain opening?

I can't recall the last time I saw a movie that started with the curtains dramatically sweeping apart as the projector chattered its images upon it.

There were no advertising slide shows to keep us occupied while we waited for the feature to begin. It was just you, your popcorn and your anticipation, staring with bated breath at an enormous drape.

When we were kids, my brother and I used to sit in the front row of the Alex Theatre. We'd pretend like we knew when the lights were dimming before the other one did, like we could make the curtain open with our will.

"It's going to open now!"

"No... now!"

"OK, really, it's opening... now!"

It's that kind of anticipation we'd also get when school let out and summer began. After nine months of structure and order, of doing what others told us to do, we were finally facing emancipation.

The freedom to sleep in so late you developed bed sores and had a hard time telling reality from dreams. Waking up each morning and wondering, "What am I going to do today?"

Swimming pool? Beach? Sandlot? Mall? Couch?

You'd leave the house with only the remotest of plans and see where the day took you. Maybe you'd end up at a friend's house who had a pool. Or the local swimming spot. The rest of the day was spent alternating between water, lounge chair and sun-warmed concrete.

Remember the sensation of the hot deck on your cold, wet back, a breeze blowing over you, making every follicle on your body light up? Your peace would soon be broken by one of your friends hopping up and down on one foot trying to get the water out of their ear.

Or a lazy day at the beach. Playing in the surf then resting on your towel, feeling your salty skin tighten as the sun evaporated the moisture off your body. You'd go home with sand in your crotch and ocean tar super-bonded to the bottom of your feet.

At least once each summer you'd get a sunburn so bad it felt like you were on fire. Simple movement became a ritual torture, and even bed was your enemy. But it always felt so good when you began to peel and your mom would scratch and pull pieces of dead skin off your back.

If we weren't in a pool, we were exploring the hills and woodlands, following deer trails or blazing our own. Sometimes we'd ride our bikes or skateboards so far away we'd have to call home to be picked up lest we not make it back in time for dinner.

Ice cream was meant to be eaten outdoors, preferably while watching the sky go from pale to cobalt blue and fading to black. Witnessing the streetlights turn on was sufficient reward for a day well-seized.

The nights were warm and long and spent with friends talking, just talking. Everything was hysterically funny or intensely serious. Maybe you'd count stars. We'd count insects being horrifically executed in the neighbor's bug zapper.

And the day wasn't over unless you came home reeking of dirt, sumac or chlorine.

Summer. When the world smells of hot asphalt, coconut lotion and dust; and time is an empty vessel you fill with your heart's desire.

When do we lose that wonder for the world? Is it when we start a career and have each day dictated for us? Is it when we have a family and live more for them then for ourselves?

Could be either, or both, or something else entirely.

But I guess the more important question is, how can we get that wonder back? Even just a little bit. Is it possible for us to wake up each day and look forward to what it will bring, wonder with excitement at what we are going to do today?

Ask yourself this: When my eyes first open in the morning and the day begins to unfold before me, do I feel a sense of drudgery? Or do I feel delight?

If it's the former, you're probably normal.

If it's the latter, you need to let us in on something.

I don't have the answer. I wish I did. But I do know that there are moments of delight, moments of wonder when everything just feels right. Those moments are where you plant your flag and claim your high ground. Isn't it amazing how those moments, however infrequent, wash away everything else?

I'm sitting in the front row, and my brother is next to me, anxious and excited. We're looking up at the curtain waiting for the lights to dim. Waiting. Anticipating. Imagining. Hoping.

OK... now!

June 12, 2010

❧

Losing a Dear Friend

I HAVE sad news to report. We've lost a beloved member of our family.

Lilly has died.

At least I'm told it was Lilly and not Poopcakes. I never could tell my daughters' goldfish apart.

But there she was, floating belly up, eyes void of life. Poopcakes swam nearby agitated, silently screaming for us to call 911. But it was too late. In fact it was bedtime, which raised even graver concerns.

My daughters, Thing 1 and Thing 2, were in the bathroom brushing teeth when I discovered the lifeless goldfish. I stood in front of the tank wondering how best to handle this, shielding them from the sight of their dead pet as they climbed into bed.

Should I take the tank out of their room now, surely attracting their attention? I could claim I was just taking them for a starlit stroll and hope to find a 24-hour pet shop to get a lookalike.

Should I tell them now that Lilly had died and risk a night of crying, lost sleep and bad dreams?

Should I turn the lights off, kiss them goodnight, then slip in like the goldfish fairy after they fell asleep, remove the corpse and leave money in its place to soften the heartache of death?

There was only one right thing to do.

"Honey," I said to the wife quietly. "Look."

I stepped away from the tank so she could see the calamity. Her eyes grew wide.

"What should we do?" I asked.

After some consideration she said, "We have to tell them."

She was right of course. She always is in such situations. I didn't want to admit what I already knew; the hardest thing to do is usually the best thing to do.

"Girls," I said. "I have some bad news."

They froze, sensing the seriousness in my tone. I lacked the appropriate words for this occasion, so I merely stepped away from the tank, revealing the shocking image of their unnaturally motionless pet atop the murky water.

Thing 1 was first to react. She brought Lilly home from the school carnival that day three years ago. Her face went white, the skin around her chin wrinkled in silent horror before the cries came like waves. The tears flowed, and she threw herself on her bed wailing.

Thing 2 stared in wonder at the tank.

"What happened?" she asked innocently.

"Lilly died," I said sadly. "I'm sorry."

"Is Poopcakes OK?"

"Yes, Poopcakes is OK."

Thing 1 looked up through red, watery eyes. Denial came first. "She's not really dead, right?"

Then anger:

"It's not fair! Why couldn't it have been Poopcakes?!"

Then bargaining: "We have to do something! I have money in my piggy bank!"

Then depression: "Why does this always happen to me? I don't deserve to be happy."

And finally acceptance: "So now can we finally get a dog?"

I raised the difficult topic of funeral arrangements. Though Lilly was old, living a longer life than we ever expected, she left no instructions for how she wanted us to handle her departure. I suggested a garden burial, near the tomato and basil plants. We'd remember her every time we had *insalata caprese*.

But Thing 1's emotions were too frayed for that. So I knew a "water burial" in the porcelain crypt was out of the question. In the end, Thing 1 didn't want to know — couldn't bear to know — what happened to her goldfish now.

I took the tank out of their room. We kissed the girls' wet cheeks and turned out the lights. We heard sniffles before the quiet blessing of sleep finally arrived.

After letting Poopcakes have a few final moments alone with her friend and life partner, I scooped Lilly out, dropped her into a baggie and laid her to rest in the trashcan outside. It sounds disrespectful, but hey, what's in that bag isn't Lilly. It's merely the vessel in which she resided. Lilly will always be with us.

She was a good pet. She never ran away, never defecated on the carpet or tore up my slippers. She never needed more than a few bites of food each day. When we forgot and let her go a few days without, she didn't complain, but greeted us with the same tail-wagging excitement that typified her character in life. Happy. Loyal. Loving. And always there for us. Always right there, in the same bowl, on the same shelf.

She is survived by her adoptive parents, Thing 1 and Thing 2, me, the wife, an extended family of aunts, uncles, grandparents and cousins, Nutty Boy the squirrel. And of course Poopcakes.

She wasn't just a goldfish. Lilly was a member in an innumerable, exclusive order: beloved first pets. She's a symbol of loving and losing, of the tides of life that cannot be held back. She will forever be the first, but sadly not the last, heart-wrenching loss in my daughters' young lives.

July 24, 2010

There's a First Time for Everything

I WAS eight. Some would say too young to understand. Others would wonder what took so long. I remember the smells, the sounds, the faces. Equally frightening and liberating. I was changed forever.

And that time has come for my daughters.

Time for Dodger baseball. Time for that pilgrimage to the Church of Chavez Ravine, the Holy Land of Hot Dogs, the temple of blue steel and gray concrete that is Dodger Stadium. The House that O'Malley Built, the Valle de Valenzuela, the land of Lasorda, the... well... you get the idea. We took Thing 1 and Thing 2 to their first Dodger game.

I remember my first time, sitting on the third-base line, my dad helping me memorize the players: Garvey, Lopes, Russell, Cey, Yeager... The infield clay a mirror reflecting the sun, the manicured grass an emerald checkerboard. I remember the line-drive foul ball striking that unsuspecting fan in the gut. Lucky fan.

I didn't expect them to be that excited. Baseball is Daddy's game. I thought they'd drag their heels going and we'd leave in the sixth inning, their attention span like most others in L.A. But I was pleasantly surprised when they donned everything blue in their wardrobe — socks, shirts, scarves, ear muffs ...

"Daddy, look! I'm even wearing blue..."

"Stop! I trust you!"

Though it's only a 10-minute drive, we leave two hours early just to restrain them in the backseat. We pay $15 to park so we can spend $200 more once inside. And since that doesn't warrant "preferred" parking, before we're even 60 feet, 6 inches in, we're ushered against our will into a lot on the opposite side of the stadium from our seats.

I'm worried less about the long walk than I am about Things 1 and 2 begging for something from each of the 500 vendors we must now pass. We eventually relent and buy each a hat, one a "#1 Fan" foam finger and the other a (gulp!) miniature baseball bat.

"You have to be careful with this. OK?"

She held it lustily, like Hannibal Lecter wielding a scalpel.

We shield their eyes past California Pizza Kitchen, Carl's Jr. and Panda Express. They can eat whatever they want when their culinary choices aren't my responsibility. We nosh on Dodger Dogs through not one, not two, but three ceremonial "first" pitches; one by a homeless shelter coordinator, the next by the sponsor of tonight's in-stadium advertising campaign and lastly an unknown actor with a movie coming to a theater near you.

I turn on my transistor radio and listen to Vin Scully on the tinny, mono AM station. It takes 30 years off us both.

"This is why I want to paint our room blue," Thing 2 tells her mother. "So we can put 'Think Blue' on the wall." That's my girl.

I cheer when the Dodgers make a play and express my frustration when they don't.

"Why are you booing, Daddy?"

I try to explain the nuances of the game.

"Well, that pitch was clearly a strike and the ump is blind." Or, "When the opposing pitcher intentionally throws the ball where the hitter can't hit it, it means he's a gutless coward and…"

"Can I get popcorn?!" she asks in a panic having spied a vendor coming down the aisle.

"You just got kettle corn!"

"Oh yeah."

I don't make them memorize the players — there will be a new roster next year anyway — but they're curious.

"Who's your favorite player, Daddy?" Thing 1 asks.

"Casey Blake. He's not flashy, shows up every day, does his job. He's a grinder. Plus he's old. Like me."

I make the trek for liquid refreshments and find a stand with no line. Then I discover why: $11 for one beer.

"I wouldn't pay it," the lonely barkeep tells me as we discuss the irony of the "family-friendly confines" during the McCourt divorce era.

"What I'm spending tonight is going to Frank's legal expenses, not pitching acquisitions," I bellow. "We're dying in the standings;

families can barely afford to get in the stadium let alone eat when they do."

And the crowd roars, but not for me. Blake hit a home run, and I missed it. Never fails. But in my good spirits I pay the beer ransom, toast the barkeep and head back to my seat.

"Daddy, your favorite guy just hit a home run! Did you see?"

"No. But I heard it."

At the seventh-inning stretch we stand, wrap our arms around one another, sway and sing as Nancy Bea Heafley leads us in song. "Root, root, root for the DODGERS…" Then the expected question comes.

"Daddy, when are we going?"

I sigh. "We can go now."

"But I want to stay until the end of the game."

She'll never know how happy she just made me.

"Why are those guys cheering for the Giants?" Thing 2 asks.

"Brain damage," I tell her. "Don't stare. It's not polite."

First times bring heirlooms, scars and luggage framed in memories. They won't remember that the Dodgers won the first time they went to a game. But will they remember the 40-foot pass from the peanut vendor? Daddy's immaculate reception? The beach balls, nachos or malts? Falling asleep with a "#1 Fan" foam finger on her headboard? Knocking the guy in front of us on the head with her mini bat?

I have no idea. But I have a few things I won't forget.

August 14, 2010

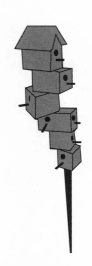

And Then

The real voyage of discovery consists
not in seeking new landscapes
but in having new eyes.

~ *Marcel Proust*

I like onions, but they don't like me.

~ *My Grandmother*

First Bird

THERE is a place in this world more lonely and frightening and life changing than any other. It is a location so hostile, so feared, people will do just about anything to detour around it. Unfortunately, it's not a rest stop or tourist attraction along some highway or atop some hill. And we can't avoid it.

It's in our mind, and its visiting hours are the middle of a sleepless night.

You find yourself there when your eyes snap open from a restless sleep and all the calamities of your life come pouring in like unwanted distant relatives at a family reunion. They're the kinfolk you don't really know too well, and you're embarrassed to admit you're related; they are the first ones at the door because they heard it was an open bar, and they are going to be the last to leave so they can take home whatever is left on the buffet.

Their names are Fear, Stress, Anxiety and Sadness. Sometimes they bring friends like Despair, Anger and Self-Loathing. They have nothing good to say about you. They are critical, opinionated and rude, and they don't care what you think about them. In fact, the more you argue with them, the more enjoyment they get out of seeing a rise in you. Their barrage is defenseless. Whether what they have to say about you is accurate or not, every negative feeling you have of yourself, your life and your circumstance in it, you can't help but admit that they are making some sense.

And in the middle of the night there is little you can do to beat them back. Every time you ask them to leave, they say, "...and one more thing..." Then they bring over a third cousin you've never met before, Hopelessness, and he wants to ask you a few questions. Or your Great Uncle Failure, who you thought had passed out under a table, woke up and wants to point out a few of your mistakes. He wants to share some things he's learned over the years just so you know what you did wrong.

Eventually the worst thing happens. In that darkness of night, surrounded by these accusing voices, when you are all alone, you start to believe them.

Everything sucks.

And it's all your fault.

You know that when the sun comes out, the veil will be torn away, and all of the horrific, self-defeating and destructive things you couldn't block out last night will be manifest in your life, as ominous and real as death, work, taxes and Sarah Palin. And everyone around you will know that you are a fake. All these mangy, scurvy distant relatives have exposed you for who you really are. Worse yet, you have to admit that you brought it all upon yourself. All the choices you made in your life have led you directly to this. You asked for it. And now you got it.

You will now be the person the entire world gets to look at and say, "Well, at least I'm not him." You'll probably end up crashing someone else's family reunion so you can feel better about yourself when you find another lowly victim to pick on with your newfound friends.

Or at least that's what it feels like.

We all wish for something meaningful from our lives. We all have hidden desires that push us through each day. Whether we admit to them or not, it's what gets us up in the morning and takes us to work; it's what gives us the strength to wipe our children's butts. Or our parent's butts. It's what allows us to get through a job we hate each day. Or even a job we're simply ambivalent about. It's what we look for when times are hard just so we can find the tiniest flicker of light in the darkness. It's a bit like the feeling you get after you buy a lottery ticket, but before you find out you didn't even get one number right; when you get permission to envision what you'll do with all that money. Only, it feels better than that.

It's hope. Or something like hope. A little chirp we feel inside telling us there is worth in the world, and in ourselves. Hope that a better job will come along. Hope that our candidate will triumph and we'll all have a better tomorrow, lower taxes, more arts in our schools and help for the homeless. Hope that all the rear-end wiping will make our kids better, more respectful human beings. Or if it's our parent's rear-ends, that our children will learn from our examples and wipe ours when the time comes. It's hope that we'll find some peace in life and finally be able to do for a living what we always dreamed we should do. Because that is what people want to wake up and do every day: "what I am meant to do." Even if we don't know exactly what that is. It is a sense of purpose. We think someone else, the universe or God, knows how we are to best fill the space between birth and death, and we're waiting for them to send us a postcard so we know where to report. The thought that we don't have a purpose in life is just too unbearable to fathom; and anyone who tells you otherwise, that they don't have this feeling at all, is soulless and in a state of apocalyptic denial. You are free to take them off your Christmas card list.

That thing I call hope or purposefulness is the internal combustion engine within each of us that never seems to stop. It may sputter and stall. It may run at high temperatures and overheat. When we're lucky it runs smoothly. But it is always running one way or another. Its fuel is our desire, that voice in our heart we can't shut up; and even when we can't see the next gas station, it is always there – around the next bend or over the next hill.

Some may have different names for it; self-preservation, intestinal fortitude, luck, synchronicity, karma, fate, destiny. That's ok. Call it what you want. It's all the same energy. It expresses itself in our lives in as many ways as there are people on this planet. That's what makes it so hard to define.

Some want to become rich in business. Others want to become rich in family. Some want to be doctors or lawyers. And others dancers, poets and painters. Some want to marry into wealth so they don't have to do anything they don't want to. And still others want nothing more than a decent job that pays the bills and will be there for years to come. It may have nothing at all to do with your job. It may be that thing you do to give you balance when you're not in the office or behind the cash register.

Me? I wanted to write. I envisioned the life of a writer as the ideal balance of work, family, creativity and business.

And then I got it.

I was handed the opportunity to write a weekly column for my local newspapers. I didn't try to get this job; I didn't send in samples for years, beat editors over the head with my pleas of desperation. I got a postcard out of the cobalt, so to speak, and I followed the directions and reported for duty, thankful I was now one of the lucky people in this world that would actually get to exercise that heart muscle.

Though I say I wanted to be a writer, I had no idea what being a writer actually meant. Nor did I even know exactly what I wanted to write beyond the newspaper column. A book? Sure. Memoir? Maybe. Short stories? OK. So, to start my writing career I was given 800 words to say whatever I wanted with the promise of dozens or thousands of readers to consume my wit and wisdom each week. And as fortune would have it, not long after taking this opportunity to write professionally, the company I worked at full time, shut its doors. The signs were all there.

Be a writer. Commit to that life and reap the rewards.

So I did.

With my wife's blessing and support, I embarked on my sabbatical year; twelve months to see if I could make a living weaving words into sentences, sentences into paragraphs, paragraphs into chapters and chapters into books. The dream job. The fulfillment of my hopes and desires. Even the ones I never knew I had.

Other benefits came with this grand life change. Besides the time to sit at my desk and wordsmith in blissful ecstasy, it afforded me time for so many other things that elude us when we're chained to a full time job.

Writing became my work priority. But without the burden of a nine-to-six, Monday-to-Friday job, I got more time for my daughters. Rather than have them in an after-school program, I was there for them. There are some wonderful programs that nurture kids between the time they leave school and the time a parent can pick them up after they get off work. But we knew that nothing replaced a parent. Now, between my wife and I, we were each be able to pick the kids up from school every day and have the extra benefit of saving hundreds of dollars each month on childcare; money we no longer had since I'd lost my full time salary.

For the first eight years of their lives, I worked full time. I saw them in the mornings, evenings and weekends, like any working parent does. But now I was there at the gate a few days each week when they got out of school. I helped them with their homework, took them to the park and on errands and mini dates. I was there for them more than I'd ever been before.

There were other people too that I wanted and needed to see more often. I didn't grow up in the same house with my father. For the majority of my life he lived too far way for me to see on a regular basis. But he'd moved into our area a few years back, within easy driving distance for breakfasts and lunches, weekend get-togethers and Dodger games. I used some of my newfound freedom to get to know him better, spending as much time with him as possible. We'd already lost so much time in the first half of my life, and it was nice to have some of that back before it was too late.

I have two nephews, and they lost their father a few years go. Well, they didn't really lose him. We know where he is: under a lovely shade tree at Forest Lawn. And they can visit him whenever they want. But with more time than I'd had before, I now had the chance to be the uncle I'd always wanted to be, something I knew they needed now more than ever.

At church I signed up to help the needy, and took part in groups of men meeting regularly to do manly things. To fellowship and grow in my faith with newfound energy.

I was able to spend time with friends. I increased my bike-riding and exercising. I spent more time with my wife and took her out on spontaneous lunch dates.

And there was more too.

More time for laundry and dishes and grocery shopping; and the cable repair appointment, car repairs and helping my elderly neighbor take groceries into her house; cleaning out the trash cans and washing cars by hand and painting hallways and window trims. And all of the other daily chores I wasn't able to do while behind a desk in an air-conditioned office.

Oh yeah, and did I mention writing?

The book, the great American novel I believed everyone had inside them, that I was supposed to have on the bestsellers list sometime halfway through my sabbatical year, did not magically appear. Shocking, I know. It was started, stopped and changed directions; started again, stopped again, thrown out. A new book was started then stopped and the ugly cycle repeated itself.

All the time one thinks they'll get if they didn't have to go to an office every day, vaporizes in the face of reality. Like a politician's integrity after Election Day.

I still wrote the column and it was going quite well. But the pay would never be enough to turn my sabbatical year into something more permanent. It was a great platform from which to launch a writing career; a built-in readership, the credibility of being a pub-lished writer, and the much-needed pressure of having to actually write each week and hone your craft. But I knew when I started this period that there would need to be something more substan-tive in my writing in order to maintain it as a lifestyle. I knew that going back to a regular job was a likely possibility at some point. But I also knew that I was doing myself and this gift a disservice if I didn't fully grasp and throttle the opportunity I was given. And such self-actualization was something I had never mastered.

There are so many things about life that one can only learn by experience. We may envision the perfect job or the perfect lifestyle. But until we've set our minds and our actions to that thing, until we've committed ourselves to walking down that path against all obstacles, we just don't have any idea what the reality is behind that vision.

Beyond the time factor, beyond finding a way to schedule myself to get some quality writing done, there is something else I had to discover, accept and understand when I put on my writing jacket and sat down at my desk to create prose as a vocation. If you've listened to those who've travelled the roads before you, you heard them say it or something like it. If you're anything like me, you just smiled and nodded when they told you; you acted like you knew what they were talking about. But you didn't listen.

Writing is a lonely craft. Some people do well by themselves, are happy left alone with their thoughts. And I have that capacity. In fact, I often relish those moments and try to create them for myself. But this bit of wisdom gets thrown out with the advice parents give their children when their children are about to become parents themselves. As a parent now, "just you wait until you have children" is a haunting prophecy I paid little heed to before I had children. The same goes for the warnings that the writing life is a treacherous path one walks alone and in one's mind.

When you write, there's no one in the next cubicle to thankfully distract you from a task you don't want to do or take off your plate. You have no boss breathing down your neck, no client expecting a project to be done on a certain date. There's no staff to support you, no one to clean out your garbage cans at night. There are no time clocks, no whistles, no Half-Day Fridays — though every day is Casual Friday.

And though some of this sounds wonderful, and can be, there's something comforting about the pressure to produce being taken off your lap; when all you need to do is what someone else tells you.

The other danger zone of writing you don't hear about so often is the isolation — which is different than simply being alone. Though you may set out to meet with friends on a regular basis, work at the coffee house a couple times each week, and even perhaps join a writing support group, at the end of the day it is just you, your mind, the keyboard and what you can pound out of each. Because when all is said and done, you're only as good as what you produce each day. If you are really devoting yourself to a writing life, you will eventually have to start shutting out the rest of the world and stop answering its calls because it is taking your attention away from what you really need to be doing. It's a balance to be sure. But it is a balance that must be found by trial and error.

And that isolation leads to something that can spin you into oblivion if you're not careful: self-examination. Whether you look into your own life as a source for your craft, or merely spend time alone in your head because you're the only one in the room, you begin to look at yourself in a way you never did before. You stop seeing yourself reflected off other people. Such solitary inward investigation can lead to a kind of mental hyperactivity that I think successful writers don't tell you about. It's that ugly, little factoid about your new job that you only discover on the first day when it's too late to back out; like the fact that the office manager is a controlling tyrant, the boss refuses to pay for coffee in the break room or that the company itself is so strapped for cash that you have to ask the CFO for copy paper one sheet at a time. There are drawbacks to your dream job that no one will share with you. Maybe they can't.

Or, if writers have told you about this little perk of the job, they appear to be speaking Urdu; you think they are trying to distract you away from something wonderful they want to keep secret. They're trying to throw you off the scent so they can preserve their own glorious and rewarding lifestyle without threat of you taking away their readers.

While some measure of isolation and self-examination can be a very healthy thing for anyone, descending into such uncharted territory can also turn a three-hour tour into seasons trapped on a desert isle with people that drive you crazy surviving on coconuts.

And if all that weren't enough, money always creeps in. The dawning reality that you aren't providing for your family, that you are contributing virtually nothing to the finances while chasing your windmills, can paralyze you. Going from being the sole bread-winner to being completely reliant on another, can destroy any faith in yourself you have left.

Sounds ideal, right?

So it was on that uncharted island I found myself midway into my sabbatical year. In the middle of the night I lay on the couch, cold sweat misting my chest, heart racing uncontrollably; my unwanted relatives Panic, Anxiety and Fear engaged in a dodge ball death match in my head.

And it wasn't just one isolated night. It was starting to happen on a regular basis.

Sleep, the last place of peace, rest and rejuvenation, was becoming dreaded territory. No matter how tired I was from consecutive sleepless nights, my eyes would pop open after only an hour's sleep and all of those filthy degenerates would stop in for a visit and tell me what they thought about my life.

You can't write. You don't make enough money and chances are you never will. Look how many people try and fail. What makes you any different than them? You're not. What kind of husband are you? What kind of a father are you? What kind of provider are you? Not a very good one, obviously. You're not a real man and have never been; a real man provides for his family. She's probably going to leave you. And she'll take the kids because you've got nothing to offer them – which is good because you've lost all patience with them anyway and they drive you crazy. You'll have to move back in with your mother. 43 years old and living in your childhood room. Maybe you can find that old Farrah Fawcett poster and put it back up over your bed. You've been out of the workforce for a while. No one will want to hire you now. Nobody who read your column this week sent you any feedback. Your audience is dwindling. The editors are probably trying to figure out how to replace you. How's the book coming along? It's not. That's right. Because you can't write a book. Sure you've been able to fake your way through the last year writing cute things about your kids or fleetingly insightful fables about life, but you're tapped out. You've got nothing left to say. No one cares what you think; you aren't a celebrity, a brilliant writer, a world traveler or a war hero. You have nothing to offer anyone.

Without even knowing it until now, I was crushed under the weight of all this. The pressure I put on myself to write something great, meaningful and profitable in one year; the frightening reality of creative endeavors where one must reside for prolonged periods in one's own head; the feelings of emasculation and servitude that come with doing daily household chores; the destroyed self confidence that comes with going from provider to dependent; the lack of income; my failings and flaws as a parent becoming so robustly obvious as a result of more time spent with the kids; watching friends take their families on trips to Europe, Hawaii and the Caribbean, while we found economy getaways within driving distance. I was overwhelmed by all of these things that I'd never experienced before and in finding that I was doing none of them with the kind of success and grace I envisioned. Not to mention the haunting guilt of knowing that my wife was working so hard to support all of us *and* doing just as much, if not more, around the house and with the kids than I was — and doing it better.

But the worst of all this was the thought of losing my family, the absolute most important thing in my life, due to my selfishness and blindness — my sunset chasing; losing my wife and children because I couldn't provide for them, and had little to show for the time I'd been given.

But here's the kicker: none of this was accurate.

Wherever it is that our fears come from, from whatever factory in this world or the next that such destruction is manufactured, it knows exactly where it can do the most damage. It knows where to hit you hardest. It was all fear, and nothing good comes from such fear; all smoke and vapors and distraction.

Those fears are not real.

Each night I'd close my eyes and feel the cool night air roll in over me from the windows above the couch, like fog cresting the hills that keep the ocean mist out of the valley, chilling my sweat-drenched body. I'd wait for the sun to bail me out, fearful I'd have to get through another day exhausted for lack of sleep.

There is a silence in the predawn hours that's hard to describe. It is an awesome and foreboding time of day; the world is pregnant, just waiting for the labor pains sunrise will bring. The city sleeps, yet there is some far off constant hum of highway travelers in the distance.

And you listen. You listen for something. Your being won't except the fact that the world can be this still, this quiet. Eventually you recognize what's missing. There is one distinct thing that is absent: birdsong. We take it for granted during the day when so many other sounds compete for our attention. But at night, in the quiet hum, the lack of birds chirping is painfully obvious. At first you wonder why the world sounds so different; then you figure it out. The melody is missing.

Eventually, from seemingly nowhere, a familiar voice rings out, shattering the silence. One bird. One bird finally works up the courage to speak; one bird decides to interrupt the solitude. It is just a simple, quiet call. But against the heaviness of night, it leaps off the tapestry.

From nothing, everything was spoken into existence. Including us. Then came the light that allows us to see the world.

After that first bird bravely sang, heralding the day, others followed.

And this happens every day before we wake. This all happens before any of us comes into being each day. One bird speaks up, cries out awkwardly, and tells us that the light is coming. Another day is coming. And with it renewal. In your job, your home, your relationships. Renewal. Time to let yesterday go and look forward to the newness of a new day. Time to embrace what unexpected things will come at you today.

It may be scary. Strike that. It is scary. It is scary to look at yourself and see that you've become complacent and lost, that you've taken the world around you, your work, your passion, your friends, your family and those you love, for granted. But I know no other way except to enter that fear knowing a song awaits you on the other side.

That's why I like that bird. I wish I were more like him.

That bird rescued me.

As the choir of birdsong mounted, the comforting sound of newspapers hitting driveways echoed out, growing near. When that soft thud reached my home, I knew the night was officially over. Relieved, yet weary of the day ahead.

Eager for the coffee that would get me through the day, I stood over the sink and let the water run while looking out the window into the backyard and beyond. The black outside turned to grey; my relatives and their friends left the party and every good thing unseen began to return. The buildings, the toys in the yard, the fence. The tree and hammock underneath its perfect shade. The bougainvillea and tomato plant. And a birdhouse. A sad, decrepit birdhouse dangling from a pole in the backyard, ready to feed and nourish every bird that came looking for life-giving, life-affirming sustenance.

Crooked Little Birdhouse

A FEW years ago I was playing with one of my daughters in the backyard, who was five years old at the time. Or rather, I was occupying myself in the garage, tinkering and organizing, while she made more mess for me to clean up. In the Suess-like, technicolor world we allow ourselves to inhabit from time to time, she's my Thing 1, and her younger sister is my Thing 2. Frenzied little creatures that seek only to delight while they bring so much mayhem around them.

While using one of my golf clubs to crush pebbles into dust, she said something that gave me a start. And thump went my heart.

"Daddy, I want to build something," she said.

She said this in the same casual way kids do when they ask for a cookie, a jet pack or a "bagillion-zillion" dollars. And it gave me the same apprehensive feeling I get when the wife asks me to dance at a wedding or when a doe-eyed three year old wants me to play dolls with her. Participation is mandatory.

My toolbox consists of a rusty hammer, several files that have never seen wood, a bent screwdriver once used to dislodge a boulder in the garden, a cheap socket set with lost pieces and one of those cone-shaped bristle devices I hear one uses to scrape the crust off car battery terminals. There is a peculiar semi-metallic-organic stench emanating from deep under everything. I don't recall ever buying any of these items. They were probably "borrowed" years ago when I moved from my parent's home. Nothing earthly can explain the smell either.

In short, I am no tool man. I drove the same truck for 16 years. Somewhere around year ten, the driver's seat broke and became a permanent recliner. I attempted to fix this myself and failed. For the remaining six years, a crate held my seat back in place, too ashamed was I to show my handiwork to a qualified repair person. I'm thankful that the guy I sold the truck to never said a word about the seat. I miss that crate though. It was a good crate.

First, I let my daughter pound nails aimlessly into a block of wood, hoping this would get the sudden carpentry urge out of her system. But five year olds bore easily. And once she's got an idea in her head, it won't go away.

So I thought about what we could build that wouldn't be, A) so complex as to frustrate her, and B) so complex as to frustrate me. In seventh grade woodshop we made aerodynamic flying ducks. But that assignment took weeks, and we young lads spent every day grinding water fowl out of a block of cedar using only sandpaper. It was a monotony I've never forgotten. And that was an age too young to fear the repercussions of carpal tunnel syndrome. I needed something to build with a twitchy adolescent in one afternoon.

There must be something in our collective subconscious that tells us the birdhouse is the simplest of all wood-making creations. I am not sure where this comes from, but it's probably the same voice that tells us ice cream has fewer calories when eaten standing at the freezer. But a birdhouse was the first thing I thought of to build. Surely the hardware store would have a kit to save me. After all, the hardware store is the E.R. of all merchants.

So we set off, Thing 1 and I. This was going to be one of those daddy-daughter moments memorialized in a Hallmark greeting card commercial, I'd determined; a day she would remember and cherish for the rest of her life. I envisioned her accepting the Nobel Prize for Carpentry, tearfully recalling our sojourns to the hardware store. The vision ends when she twists her genetically inherited weak ankle falling offstage, streaming the expletives also learned from me in our years of woodworking together.

Normally I like to go to the hardware store alone. I wander without purpose, beginning with the barbecues and grilling equipment. Open a few lids until I feel one with just the right weight; resent how many more square inches of surface grilling space this one has than mine at home. And let's not even talk about the BTU's.

Then I'll amble through the gardening section and imagine transforming my backyard into Eden. A few new flower beds, compost pile and one huge area with every fruit tree, vegetable and herb my family could possibly need to live sustainably from for the rest of our lives. I will provide.

Then there's the home organizing aisle. Here I foresee a hook, basket, shelf, cubby, cabinet and roll-away storage bin for everything in the house and garage. Perfect organization is achievable in my mind, and here is the answer.

But today we have a goal. We know what we need. I shop like I drive: I know how to get there, no matter where "there" is, and I won't stop for directions. But nowhere, can I find a birdhouse kit.

We find birdseed, and indeed birdhouses, but no kits to build one. So, as I had feared, and somewhere deep down hoped, we'll have to build our birdhouse from scratch. And I am now determined to make it better than any kit.

After some pacing up and down the lumber aisle with Thing I intoning, "This one looks nice, Daddy. This one looks nice, Daddy. This one looks nice, Daddy," I finally select a couple pine planks, mostly for their limited knots. What moles are to smooth skin, knots are to wooden boards.

I grab a box of nails, then a dowel to use for perches. Thing I immediately grabs the dowel from my hand.

"Can I see the stick, Daddy?"

"It's not a stick, honey. It's a dowel."

And before I can tell her to be careful, she's already stabbing unsuspecting customers with it. I apologize to them as we hurriedly make our way to the register. And here she spies a hammer made just for her. It's small and pink with pretty flowers and glitter all over it. A must-have – in her eyes. I buy it for her, knowing it will be safer for her to use this than a real hammer.

At home, I haven't even gotten the lumber out of the car yet when she's already chiming like an alarm clock.

"What can I do, Daddy? What can I do? Daddy, what can I do? Daddy, Daddy, Daddy? What can I do, Daddy?"

Distraction is one of the fundamental tools in a parent's war chest.

I tell her she needs to practice with her new hammer before we can start anything.

"It's like a virtuoso's violin," I tell her. "You must become one with it."

She brings it to her lips, kisses it, and holds it lovingly against her cheek.

I pull out an old piece of scrap wood, place it in the middle of the driveway with a handful of tacks, and let her have at it.

I now have maybe two minutes in which to design the birdhouse without her "help." I go through a series of blueprints in my head, scaling down as I go. Then I settle on the simplest design I can envision. In my mind it's a three-walled room; a cube with one side missing.

I set to cutting one of the planks into equal sections. Thing I assists by holding the newly cut pieces as they are about to fall. We then sit on the ground and begin hammering. I place each nail and start it with a tap, then let her attempt to pound it the rest of the way.

After 20 minutes and three bent nails, she notices a grasshopper on the watering can, drops her hammer and walks away.

This is now my project.

Left to my own, I fall blissfully into the Zen of doing something with my hands. I pound nails and drift deeper into my own world, leaving my backyard in peaceful, transcendental meditation. The sun is shining, there is a light breeze, the kids are occupied, and all is as it should be. I finish the birdhouse.

The first thing I notice is that it doesn't sit flat. Then I notice that the roof bevels, opposite corners rising to sloping, awkward peaks. Light passes through the seams between wall and roof in places.

My birdhouse is crooked.

And I am disappointed. I didn't set out to make a perfect birdhouse or a mansion for my avian friends. But I certainly wasn't expecting it to look this... well... sad. It didn't take a whole lot of effort to make, but the result is far less than what I'd hoped. Not only am I ashamed of it, but I am ashamed of myself. This unappealing, unshapely and unattractive thing is the best I could do.

Nonetheless, the family gathers for the mounting ceremony. The girls "ooh" and "aah" as if they were at a fireworks show; the wife tells us how nice it looks. I could shoot 200 on the golf course and she'd still tell me how great I did. But I gladly accept her praise anyway. I'm convinced that all men are simply boys who need at least one "attaboy" every day. Failure to get said praise results in unexplained episodes of road rage and beer-induced acts of bravado. Whenever you see a grown man attempting to ride a skateboard in one of those funny home videos on TV, that's a man who didn't get his "attaboy" today.

We mount the birdhouse on a post to one side of the backyard. Each daughter throws a handful of birdseed into it, and we all sit back waiting for grateful finches and doves to sup on the bounty we've provided.

And we wait.

Soon the daughters pick up my tape measure and wander off to measure the fence, the sidewalk, some twigs and themselves. Eventually the wife and I give up as well. If I wanted to see some evidence of a bird, I should have washed my car.

So the birdhouse sits out in the backyard, and for the next few days we notice that the seed is missing. This gives me some satisfaction. I am contented to know that, even if I haven't seen them, little birdies are surviving another day due to my benevolence.

One afternoon, we decided to have dinner outside with the kids. I'd just put some more seed into the birdhouse, and we sat down to eat. The bent roof and ill-fitting seams don't bother me much anymore. And now we're starting to actually get some birds to visit our crooked little birdhouse.

And that's when we see something else.

Out of the corner of my eye, I see a dark figure dart from behind the bougainvillea, stop at the base of the birdhouse post, then quickly shimmy up to the top.

Rats.

The birds scatter as a rat sits inside the birdhouse taking in a fine meal of sunflower seeds and dried corn.

We're aghast; disgusted. And these aren't just rats. These are the kinds of vermin you see in documentaries about New York's sewer system. Big and brave, each with a pack of cigarettes rolled up in its sleeve. One after another comes out of hiding and climbs up to overtake the birdhouse.

As the rats come and go I try to figure out what to do. I feel bad for the displaced birds. I'd built this sanctuary for them and they're being evicted by this scourge. But I feel even worse for myself. In my melancholy I wonder why it didn't work out. Where did I go wrong? What did I do to let them down? What failure or core incompetence in my life caused me to be so incapable of doing this successfully? In my vision of the birdhouse there were only happy, grateful birds. Like the mechanical one that has a duet with Mary Poppins.

But as the rats glutton themselves, I notice something else. The scurrying, sceavy creatures scatter seed to the ground as they make merry in the birdhouse. The birds see this and dive in to claim whatever falls out, unaware of just how wrong this situation is or how unjustly they've been treated. Each time the rats leave the bird-house for a moment, the birds retake it and move on.

The birds seem to be dealing with this incursion a lot better than I am.

This whole rats-in-the-birdhouse situation troubles me for days. I don't ask for much. I've never been a person who wanted a lot of new toys and material wealth. I've always been happy with simple pleasures. My office jobs have always been decent though spiritually draining at times, like any job. I have dreams but feel like I'm incapable of achieving them – or prevented from doing so by unseen and Machiavellian forces. Sure the kids are healthy, but there's so much I want to give them that I simply can't.

Can nothing be left sacred? Can't I have just this one thing to peacefully enjoy without disturbance? Can there be one part of my life that is off-limits to the slow, eroding forces of this world?

And the answer came back.

No.

Everything is crooked.

That birdhouse, my house, the house I grew up in, my life, my job, my faith, everyone's life. They are all crooked.

And we all have rats.

I grew up in a nice neighborhood near a golf course in the hills just outside Los Angeles. It was a quiet, secluded and idyllic suburban world. We lived in a large house on a dead end street with very little traffic. The kids of the neighborhood could play unattended all day in the streets; kickball, baseball, bikes, kites, with only the occasional call — "car!" — to snap us out of our daydream. When we felt adventurous, we'd climb into the unscarred hills of our backyard, building forts within overgrown sumac forests, carving bunkers and foxholes out of dirt embankments. Or, we'd venture onto the golf course on Mondays, the day it was closed, and slog through the creeks catching pollywogs and seeing who could find the most lost golf balls.

We were a happy family from the eyes of its youngest child. But I see now the crooked walls and ill-fitting seams. Rats got in. There was infidelity and divorce, addiction and rebellion, fights and frustration between two step-families trying to coexist when my mother remarried. I'm sure there were money struggles too, although I never witnessed them firsthand — unless you count the time I wanted a new bike and was turned down. This is when I learned that writing a check did not mean creating money one didn't have.

Dad was off starting a family with his new wife. My childhood vision of my father is the man we went to visit for a weekend every few months and a week in the summer. He was the guy who hadn't sent the check yet whenever I wanted a new bike.

Though I am as happily married as the next person, probably more so, like my childhood home, the home I've made with my wife and children has its rats. There are disagreements, financial concerns, misunderstandings and annoyances. The kinds of things every relationship must contend with at some time or another. I have a tendency to repeat the same nostalgic story from my youth, thinking I've never told my wife this one before. She just smiles and nods now.

There is never enough money or time. The carpet in the living room is an ugly green, and there are smelly spots where spilled milk is still fermenting. I want more time with the family. When I get more time with the family, I want more time away from the family.

Yet somehow we're happy — above-average happy when we survey the world around us, rats and all.

On Sundays we go to church where we're told just how crooked our birdhouse *really* is.

As a churchgoer, I am supposed to live by a manifesto of irrefutable rules and definitions about the correct way to conduct myself in this world. This set of standards is like a duffel bag I lug through the airport as I wait for my flight to finally take off. I am supposed to be a good person, give to the needy, refrain from sinning, do unto others, lead a godly life. As if that were really possible.

Though it can be an unpopular view, I believe in God the creator, in Jesus his son sent to atone for the mess we've made of this place and offering a way out. I believe in the Holy Spirit that works minor and major miracles around us each and every day. I pray. I hope. I try to listen and learn and have patience and reverence and humility. I ask for forgiveness when I screw up, and I occasionally remember to say thank you when it strikes me that something has gone right. But not near enough. So I guess that makes me a Christian — just a garden variety, generic, plain wrap Christian. Not a catholic or a Presbyterian or a Methodist or a Baptist or a Lutheran. Just a Christian. But I do consider myself a challenged Christian. And here's why.

I swear. I drop curse words in my daily dialogue like rotten fruit falling from an untended lemon tree.

I drink. Occasionally and recreationally. But, not as much as I did in my youth. As I get older, I appreciate the finer spirits, premium wines, expensive sipping tequila and a smoky, golden Scotch aged in sherry oak casks. Sometimes, if the company and libations are of high quality, I'll drink just a little too much; enough to regret it the next day on rare and random occasions.

When I get my haircut, I sneak a peek at the Playboy magazine just sitting there, calling me, beckoning me. Just for the articles of course. And I'm a little disappointed when the wait isn't very long.

I don't care when the earth was created or how. We're here on it and need to worry more about caring for it because that's what we were instructed to do. I don't always have the perfect bible verse for any given situation on the tip of my tongue. "The End" may be coming soon, but I can't live my life looking for signs, reading subversive plots into global and local political events, or worrying what you hear when you play Supertramp's "Breakfast in America" backwards.

I don't think Fox News, Glenn Beck, Bill O'Reilly, Sean Hannity and Ann Coulter know any more than I do or have tapped into some mineral vein of truth the rest of us just aren't wise or clearminded enough to get on our own.

The church itself is a crooked birdhouse. It's done a good job over the centuries of building beautiful temples and elaborate cathedrals; the good news preached over the last 2000 years has been a salvation and sanctuary for all mankind. But if the church is the body of Christ, somebody needs to call an ambulance. And if we're all created in God's image, what does that say about our maker? When I sit in the pews I'm surrounded by misfits and miscreants, thieves, addicts, corruptors, vixens, harlots and lotharios; murderers, bastards, idiots, angry old curs and crones; the homosexual, asexual and perversely sexual; the selfish, the contemptible, the mean and the bitter.

In short, the church body is you and me.

And maybe that's why I go. It's hard not to feel better about myself when I'm amidst several hundred of the worst singers I've ever heard, unabashedly lifting their voices in one around me. I'm in right company.

Society is crooked. The media is crooked. Politics is crooked. Humanity is crooked.

Pollution, wars, famine, child soldiers in Africa, elder abuse down the street, abortion, Sarah Jessica Parker movies. Ryan Seacrest got a star on the Hollywood Walk of Fame before Dennis Hopper did. What further evidence do you need?

We pop pills too much but don't drink enough water. And when we do drink water, we throw the plastic bottles into a landfill. We live in the most populated world in history, yet hide from each other physically and emotionally. I've isolated myself behind a computer or a window at the Taco Bell drive-thru; behind a hedge to avoid my neighbor, behind dark, mirrored sunglasses that prevent anyone from seeing into my soul, behind a façade of self confidence, control and wisdom.

And I wonder every day. Is everyone else hiding too?

We worship fame and celebrity. We idolize self-anointed experts on image, politics, culture, love, relationships and health who dictate what is beautiful and important. We find the voice on TV or radio that agrees with our own and deny all others. Entertainment has replaced information. The truth is relevant to the circumstance. We're more interested in defining and hardening our differences than embracing and glorifying our similarities. And there is a lot more that unites us than separates us.

I don't care if you believe in a different god or gods than I do or none at all. But do you have faith in something?

I don't care who you voted for, who you podcast or which pundit your TiVO is set to record each day. Who did you talk to when you were really down? When you were really happy?

I don't care if you saw George Clooney at Musso & Frank or if your friend's cousin is a dog-walker for Brangelina. Did you see your kid up on stage at the school Christmas pageant?

We all suffer and struggle, question and doubt ourselves. We scratch our way to the end of the day and the blessing of dreams. That is, if we can get to sleep and stay asleep.

I force myself to believe that everyone else feels as lost and frustrated and scared as I do. I believe that because, if I didn't, if I was truly alone on this side of the dodge ball court, such isolation would be more than I could handle.

We're all trying to make some sense of it all, and we all have a different way of expressing that one unifying thing. The rest is wasted energy.

Cheap lumber.
Poor construction.
Rats.
Broken dreams.
Unfulfilled promise.
Wasted time.
Misplaced importance.
Crooked birdhouses.

Crooked Little Birdhouse

I can't create my own world, though I try to every day of my life. I can't force this world, my home, my church, even myself, to fit into some image of my creation. The world I'm in is the only one I get. And it is a crooked world, bent, damaged, corroded, shabby, awkward and scary. Try as I might to make the people around me, the world around me, even you reading this right now, fit into some vision of purpose and orderliness, it's just not possible. Not only is it not possible, it's not the way things are supposed to be.

But this world and the people in it supply me with everything I need. There is so much beauty, so many wonders for us to discover and relish and be grateful for. Like seeds scattered in the grass. I believe that is what we're meant for, what our collective purpose is.

Finding peace with each other is almost as important as finding peace within ourselves. Every venomous thing we hurl at others is merely a symbol of something inside ourselves that is not right. And every venomous thing thrown at us, is just a similar internal wound for the one who hurls it.

The birds don't mind the rats and the aesthetically displeasing design of the walls and roof. They are fed. In that, I find great beauty — and every once in a while, some peace of mind.

The sun has warped the untreated wood turning it sickly gray. The perches snapped off in one of many falls. The seams grow wider as does the bending slope of the roof. But I love this sad, crooked birdhouse. The birds keep coming. They don't seem to mind the flawed home I've provided for them. Maybe that's what makes it, make us, full of life, desperate and colorful, different and the same. And overwhelmingly amazing.

I'm humbled by the perfection of it all. The perfection of imperfection.

After

AS I sat to write these words, I realized that it was exactly one year to the day since I was laid off from my "regular" job and decided to call myself a writer.

Except for the essays you hold in your hands, "The Book," the one I believe we all have in us, is still in progress. It unfolds itself a little each day. I continue to write the newspaper column, and have several other projects that grip me and won't let me go. I'm not sure if any will get completed, but I'm going to keep trying.

So what am I left with? Besides one essay for each week printed in the local newspaper, what do I have to show? Not much that can be quantified, monetized or realized.

I am still married to the most amazing woman I have ever met. A woman who surprises me every day; who keeps me alive with her love, her energy and her lust for life; a woman who makes my world rich in ways she'll never know.

I have the most precious and vibrant and supernaturally beautiful daughters any man could ask for. They are the greatest thing I have ever taken part in creating. Two daughters who, when other kids talk about what their father's do, will never know how awesome they make me feel when they reply proudly that their father is an "article writer."

And I am left with lessons. In this, my sabbatical year, I've learned. My, have I learned.

I learned that men get far too much credit for doing even the smallest domestic or parental chore; for doing any of the things women have done forever, but doing them not nearly so well.

While my wife works long hours, mothers her children and puts up with her husband with more grace, guts and humanity than I can fathom, I get praise for simply being a man who takes his kids to school, picks them up and makes dinner three days each week. For doing the things just a fraction as competently as she'd done all by herself when I worked out of the house, I am fawned over as a great man. I need to do little else to earn accolades. Even my best weeks of writing earned me less praise than simply getting my daughters dressed in the morning. Now mind you, I'm a firm believer that being available and present for one's children is in itself an enormous accomplishment and something so necessary for a healthy family. But, there is something wrong about our culture that it praises men so greatly for doing so much less at home than their wives have always done.

I learned that being home with the kids is harder work than anything anyone can do out of the house full time. And that's putting it mildly. It's like doing open heart surgery on yourself. Your life is in your own hands, because your heart is outside your body. It's in your children, in your spouse, in the home you are trying to maintain for them. And every calamity that befalls them, every bruise, every disappointment, every emotional hurdle, hurts you tenfold. And much of the time it is you that is inflicting those wounds; due to your selfishness, short-temperedness, confusion, frustration, blindness; your vanities, your foolish desires and visions of perfection.

I learned that, "Because I said so," is an absolutely valid answer to any of the hundreds of "whys?" a parent gets asked in a day.

I learned that being there for your kids mostly means breaking up fights, getting snacks, picking up clothes, arguing, demanding, crying, apologizing and feeling like a failure

But the greeting card moments do come. You just have to make sure you're clear-minded enough to grasp them when they do.

I learned that I'd been taking my self-worth, self-image and self-confidence, from everyone around me; my wife, my kids, my family, friends, coworkers, bosses and anyone who read my work. Relying on others to approve of you and assure you that you are all right is unfair to them and unhealthy for you. You can't set others to live up to your expectations, standards and needs. You have to find in yourself that which gives you value and worth in this world.

I learned that God is gracious enough to give you what you ask for sometimes. Even if he knows it's not the best thing for you. He delights in seeing us make discoveries, which is why he doesn't tell us exactly what to do or where the treasures are hidden. He weeps for us more than we could ever know when we are in pain. And he rejoices with a delight unmeasured when we grow, succeed and find our purpose. I know this because I am a parent. And my children have no idea that I feel this same way about them.

I learned that your purpose and your passion may not necessarily be your profession. I thought I wanted to be a writer. And I still do. But, after going into the fear, into the thing that scared me the most, I learned that my passion and my purpose are actually loving and providing for my family. Everything else is secondary.

I'm still going to write. I learned that I can do it with passable competency. But is it my profession? That remains to be seen. If I can take care of my family as a writer, so be it. If not, it won't stop me from writing. I know now that I have a responsibility to this gift to sit down whenever I can and be the first bird; to say something, to speak into the darkness and hope that others hear, and know that they are not alone.

I learned that silk and wool are not machine washable, and, when in doubt, one should set them aside and ask.

I learned that I can't create a perfect birdhouse. Or a perfect world. And that life is about finding the good, true and eternal amidst all the chaos.

Acknowledgments

Let me just get this out of the way first. Nothing, not this book, my life, my achievements, the love of my family and friends, absolutely nothing, would be possible without God. So I give him thanks first. You rock.

Now, having said that, there are a few mortals without whom this book and the stories within it would not have been humanly possible. My eternal, heartfelt and sincere thanks go to...

Karen, the least of what you are to me is The Wife. You are my muse, my best friend, my partner in crime, my test kitchen and the love of my life. Thank you for your devoted support through this and for sharing this life with me. Chloe and Emily, the source of my greatest happiness and never-ending fodder for material to write about. You teach me how to be a better person. I know one day you will find out why strangers ask you which one of you is Thing 1 and Thing 2. And on that day you will be very mad at me. But know that everything I do is out of love for you. Darlene Hubanks, for living for your children before yourself. You are a great teacher and an amazing mother. Bob Caneday, for teaching me so many more life lessons than you know you did. I hope you know how much you mean to me. Byron Hubanks and Nancy Caneday, thank you for your friendship throughout my life and for loving my parents. Chris, Lisa and Mike, we are four siblings with four unique stories. And my story wouldn't be complete without you. Randy Broadrick, Saul Serna, Lauris Bye, Maurice Delgado and Tina Briones, the closest and best friends a person could ever ask for. You don't know how much you guys mean to me. But I do. Scott and Kiersten Hathcock for their friendship, encouragement and wine in "the lounge" while the kids played. Danette Goulet, the editor who would not let me say no to writing the Small Wonders column, and to Dan Evans, the editor who has supported it and me ever since. I never would have done this if not for your belief in my writing and the freedom you give me. Thank you, Jason Wells and the entire staff at the Los Angeles Times Community News Division.

Al Martinez, the lion of Los Angeles columnists, you took me under your wing, supported, encouraged and mentored me. If I become half the writer you are, my life will be complete. M. Brent Edmund (thewriterpro.com) provided editorial services on the essays in this book and I am so grateful for his eyes and mind. Gregory Mandallaz let me sit at his coffee house for endless hours, taking the prime table away from other customers for the price of a café latte. Most of this book was written at Simply Coffee. To the faithful readers of the Small Wonders column, seriously folks, I don't know what I'm doing. But week after week you continue to read my column and say nice things to me. Writers are naturally self-doubting, and every week you lift me up. Thank you. And I am so thankful for the generous support of everyone who contributed through Kickstarter to making this book a reality, including: Sylvie Madore, Marguerite Beck, Robert Briones, Susan Koury, Conny Goodreau, Barbara LaWall, Onno Hoogendoorn, Andrew Caneday, Sean Welch, Lennox Milne, J. Christopher Nastro, Brit Trydal and Bill Nicoll, Christine Whitton and Jim and Maria Kerrigan.

All Small Wonders columns in this book were first published in the Glendale News Press and Burbank Leader. Grateful acknowledgement is given to them and their parent company, The Los Angeles Times.

About the Author

Patrick Caneday is the writer of the Small Wonders column appearing in several Southern California newspapers each week. He was raised in Glendale, California, and now lives in neighboring Burbank. He worked in the entertainment industry as a post-production supervisor and executive before taking his sabbatical year to be a writer and house-dad. He now focuses most of his time on family, his column and other writing projects. He may be reached at www.patrickcaneday.com and patrickcaneday@gmail.com.

Cover design by Alistair Milne
www.brightgreenshirt.com

Made in the USA
Charleston, SC
15 April 2011